COMFORT FOODS

Comfort Foods

Rachael Ray's
30-MINUTE MEALS

Contents

Introduction

I was a lucky little kid in many ways, but when it comes to food, I realize now that I was in the top percentile of the luckiest kids on the planet.

I literally grew up in kitchens, at home and in restaurants. I can remember being balanced on my mama's hip as she stirred big pots on the stove while in lively conversation with three different people..Then, as now, food meant family, lots of good company, happy moments together.

As I grew older, cooking became a natural form of self expression; it was great to work behind the stove. Then rather unexpectedly I discovered the satisfactions of teaching. My current passion is to take the foods I love — comfort, gourmet, vegetarian (the list is long) — and develop quick and healthy dishes that anyone can successfully prepare in 30 minutes or less.

Comfort foods, I'm happy to say, are easier to prepare than one thinks. In less time than it takes Domino's to deliver, you can have homemade Meatloaf Patties and Smashed Potatoes, classic Chicken Fricassee, hearty Red Beans and Rice or creamy New England Clam Chowder. And it's all fresh, made of quality ingredients, economical, and always delicious.

For me, developing and teaching The 30-Minute Meal is like playing a game show: the better your results, the bigger my grand prize. Whenever someone stops to tell me how these 30-Minute Meals make their lives a little richer, their words truly make me light up inside.

Cooking brings me joy because it allows me to share something of myself with those I love. It will do the same for you.

Enjoy!

Rachael Ray

Soups, Stews, and One-Pot Meals

Fall. Now here's a season! Mountains on fire with color: red, orange, yellow, brown, and burgundy—the whole Crayola box! And does life get any better than apple-picking, slow-dancing under a low harvest moon, or a great meal after home-coming?

Cider donuts, beef stew, corn chowder, and pumpkin anything are my favorite comfort foods of the season. Indulge yourself, and keep that soup pot simmering!

North Country Corn Chowder

SERVES 6

3 tablespoons corn or other vegetable oil
   (3 turns around the pan)
3 medium white potatoes, peeled and diced
1 medium onion, chopped
3 stalks celery from heart of stalk, chopped
1 small red bell pepper, seeded and chopped
2 bay leaves, fresh or dried
1 tablespoon Old Bay seasoning (half a palmful)
Coarse salt and black pepper, to taste
3 tablespoons all-purpose flour (a handful)
1 package (10 ounces) frozen corn kernels,
   defrosted and drained
1 can (15 ounces) vegetable or chicken broth
1 quart whole milk or 1% low-fat milk
4 scallions, chopped, to garnish
Oyster crackers, for topping

Heat a deep pot over medium to medium-high heat. Add oil and potatoes. Cover and cook 5 minutes, stirring frequently.

Add onion, celery, red bell pepper, and bay leaves. Season with Old Bay and salt and pepper. Cover and reduce heat a bit; cook a few minutes more, stirring occasionally.

Uncover and whisk in flour. Cook a minute more. Add corn, chicken broth, and milk. Bring soup to a boil, reduce heat, and simmer, 7 to 10 minutes, to thicken. Adjust seasonings and serve bowls of chowder with a sprinkle of chopped scallions and oyster crackers.

Homemade Chicken and Stars Soup
SERVES 4

2 quarts (8 cups) chicken broth

1 pound boneless, skinless chicken breast or
chicken tenders

1 bay leaf, fresh or dried

2 medium carrots, peeled and chopped or
thinly sliced

2 stalks celery from heart of the stalk, chopped

1 medium onion, finely chopped

1 cup star-shaped egg pastina pasta (about half
a 12-ounce box or bag)

Ground black pepper, to taste

Suggested garnishes: grated Parmigiano or
Romano cheese, chopped fresh flat-leaf
parsley, oyster crackers, crushed saltines,
croutons, plain popcorn or white cheddar
popcorn

Heat 1 quart (4 cups) broth to boiling, add chicken and bay leaf to pot, and simmer, covered, for about 8 minutes. Add vegetables to pot when you finish chopping each of them. Remove chicken meat after 8 minutes and place on a cutting board to cool.

Add the second quart of broth to your pot and bring liquid to a boil. Add pasta and cook 6 minutes. Remove soup pot from heat. Dice chicken and add to soup. Season soup with pepper to taste. If soup is too thick, add up to 2 cups of water to achieve desired consistency. Top with your choice of garnishes.

Italian Wedding Soup
SERVES UP TO 4

2 tablespoons extra-virgin olive oil (two turns
  around the pan)
2 carrots, peeled and chopped
2 celery stalks from heart of stalk, chopped
1 medium onion, chopped
2 bay leaves, fresh or dried
3/4 pound ground veal, or ground beef, pork,
  and veal mixture
1 egg, beaten
1/2 cup plain bread crumbs (a couple of handfuls)
1/3 cup grated Parmigiano or Romano cheese
  (a handful)
2 pinches ground nutmeg (1/4 teaspoon)
Salt and pepper, to taste
1 quart (32 ounces) chicken broth
2 cups warm water
1 cup dried pasta (broken up fettuccini, ditalini,
  rings, egg pasta—whatever you like)
A handful chopped fresh flat-leaf parsley, or
  2 teaspoons dried

Extra grated cheese, for the table
Crusty Italian bread, for dipping

In a deep pot heat olive oil over medium heat.
Add chopped vegetables and bay leaves.
Cover pot and cook 5 or 6 minutes, stirring
occasionally.

While the veggies cook, combine ground meat
with egg, bread crumbs, cheese, nutmeg, and
salt and pepper.

Uncover veggies, add broth and water, and
raise heat to high. Bring liquids to a boil. Roll
meat mixture into bite-size meatballs and drop
into boiling broth. Add pasta. Return to a boil.
Reduce heat and simmer 8 minutes, until pasta
is al dente and meatballs are cooked
through—split one open and make sure there
is no pink left in the meat. Add parsley and
remove from heat.

Serve soup in shallow bowls with grated cheese
and bread.

Navy Bean and Bacon Soup

SERVES 4

1 tablespoon extra-virgin olive or other
    vegetable oil (once around the pan)
6 slices lean bacon, chopped ("center cut" or
    "hearty thick" style)
2 medium white potatoes, peeled and diced
1 medium onion, chopped
2 stalks celery from the heart of the stalk,
    chopped
2 carrots, peeled and chopped
2 bay leaves, fresh or dried
3 or 4 pinches cayenne pepper
3 cans (15 ounces each) Great Northern white
    beans, drained
1 quart (32 ounces) chicken broth
1/2 cup smoky barbecue sauce
Coarse black pepper, to taste
Oyster crackers or seasoned croutons, to
    garnish

Heat oil in deep pot over medium-high heat. Add bacon and cook 3 to 5 minutes to brown, stirring frequently. Add potatoes and cook 3 minutes more. Add onion, celery, carrots, bay leaves, and cayenne. Reduce heat to medium. Cover pot and cook 5 minutes, stirring occasionally.

Add beans, chicken broth, and barbecue sauce. Bring soup to a boil, reduce heat, and simmer till potatoes are tender. Season with black pepper to taste. Sprinkle soup with oyster crackers or croutons to garnish.

Cheddar Cheese Soup

SERVES UP TO 6

3 pats butter (2 to 3 tablespoons)

1 medium onion, chopped

3 scallions, sliced thin

1 stalk celery, chopped fine

1 bay leaf, fresh or dried

3 tablespoons all-purpose flour (a handful)

3 pinches ground nutmeg (1/8 teaspoon)

2 cups chicken broth

1 quart whole milk or 2 percent milk

2 1/4 cups shredded sharp cheddar cheese

4 dashes Worcestershire sauce

Salt and pepper, to taste

12 blades fresh chives, chopped

Melt butter in a deep pot over medium heat. Add onion, scallions, celery, and bay leaf. Sauté vegetables 2 minutes, until onions are translucent. Sprinkle in flour and nutmeg and stir to blend. Cook 2 minutes more. Add broth, stir, and bring to a boil. Lower heat and simmer 5 minutes. Add milk. Heat to a boil again, then add cheese. Stir until cheese melts into soup. Add Worcestershire sauce and season with salt and pepper to taste. Garnish soup with chopped chives.

A BLT sandwich makes a great partner to this soup.

French Onion Soup, Bistro Style

SERVES UP TO 4

3 tablespoons butter

6 large sweet onions, such as Vidalia or Texas
    Sweet, sliced very thin

Salt and pepper, to taste

1/2 teaspoon ground thyme or poultry seasoning

2 cups beef broth

1 cup chicken broth

1 cup water

1/2 cup dry sherry

1 bay leaf, fresh or dried

1/4 cup heavy (whipping) cream

1 cup shredded Gruyère or smoked Gruyère
    cheese

4 slices stale French bread, toasted

Chopped fresh thyme or chives, to garnish

Heat a large, deep pot over medium to medium-high heat. Melt butter in pot and add onions. Season with salt and pepper and thyme or poultry seasoning. Cook onions down until they caramelize, turning sweet, soft, and golden brown, 20 to 25 minutes.

While onions cook, place broths, water, and sherry in another saucepot with bay leaf and bring to a boil. Reduce heat to low and simmer until onions have browned.

Add boiling broths to onions, then stir in cream. Adjust seasonings to taste. Remove from heat.

Pile grated gruyère on toasted French bread slices and place under broiler until cheese bubbles and edges are brown.

Ladle soup into bowls and, using a spatula, top bowls with cheese toasts. Garnish with chopped fresh thyme or chives.

Minestra
(Beans and Greens)

SERVES 6

MEAT-FREE MINESTRA

1/4 cup extra-virgin olive oil (3 turns around
　　the pan)

8 cloves garlic, chopped

1 medium onion, chopped

2 medium heads escarole greens (1 1/4 to 1 1/2
　　pounds), washed, dried, and coarsely chopped

3 cans (14 1/2 ounces each) cannellini beans,
　　drained

1 quart (32 ounces) vegetable broth

1/2 teaspoon ground nutmeg (3 or 4 pinches)

Coarse salt and black pepper, to taste

Lots of grated Parmigiano, Romano, or Asiago
　　cheese, for the table

Warm crusty bread, for sopping and mopping
　　up plates

MINESTRA WITH MEAT

Substitute chicken broth for vegetable broth
and add the following to above ingredients list:

1/4 pound pancetta (Italian rolled, cured pork
　　from deli counter), or 1/4 pound center-cut
　　bacon, chopped

1/4 pound prosciutto, chopped

1/4 pound capocollo ham, chopped

Heat a deep skillet over medium heat. Add oil and garlic. When garlic speaks by sizzling in oil, add onion and meats, if you are using them. Sauté onion or onion and meats for 5 minutes.

Add escarole and turn the greens with tongs until they are completely wilted. Add beans and vegetable or chicken broth. Sprinkle nutmeg, salt, and pepper into your beans and greens; stir in. Partially cover pot and let greens cook 10 minutes.

Serve with lots of grated cheese and warm, crusty bread.

New England Clam Chowder
SERVES 2 TO 3

2 tablespoons butter

1 small onion, chopped fine

1 bay leaf, fresh or dried

2 tablespoons flour (a handful)

1 rounded teaspoon Old Bay seasoning
   (1/3 palmful)

1 cup clam juice

1 can (14 ounces) low-sodium chicken or
   vegetable broth

2 cups whole milk or light cream

2 medium white-skinned potatoes, peeled
   and diced

1 can (10 ounces) baby or chopped clams,
   drained

Coarse salt and black pepper, to taste

Chopped fresh chives, to garnish

Oyster crackers, to garnish

In a deep pot, melt butter over medium heat. Add onion and bay leaf and cook 2 or 3 minutes. Whisk in flour and Old Bay and cook 2 minutes more. Whisk in clam juice and broth and combine; cook until broth begins to thicken. Stir in milk slowly. Add potatoes, raise heat to high, and bring soup to a boil. Reduce heat to a simmer and cook, 12 to 15 minutes till potatoes are tender. Add clams and heat through, 2 to 3 minutes. Season with salt and pepper.

Serve soup with chives and oyster crackers, to garnish.

French Country Chicken and Sausage Soup

SERVES 4

Based on the classic French dish cassoulet, this hearty soup combines sausage, chicken, and white beans.

3/4 pound sweet sausage, in bulk, or remove links from casings

2 tablespoons extra-virgin olive oil (twice around the pan), plus a drizzle for browning meat

3/4 pound boneless, skinless chicken breast or thigh meat, diced

1 bulb fresh fennel, trimmed of tops and chopped

1 large yellow-skinned onion, peeled and chopped

4 cloves garlic, cracked and broken away from skin by whacking against the flat of a large knife

1 bay leaf, fresh or dried

1 can (15 ounces) Great Northern white beans, drained

1 can (15 ounces) diced tomatoes

1 quart (32 ounces) chicken broth

2 tablespoons fresh rosemary, chopped (a couple of fresh sprigs), or 1 teaspoon dried rosemary, crushed in palm of hand

2 tablespoons fresh thyme, chopped (the yield of a few sprigs), or 1 teaspoon dried thyme leaves, crushed in palm

Black pepper, to taste

Garlic bread or garlic croutons, for topping soup

In a deep pot, brown sausage in a touch of olive oil over high heat. Remove sausage and drain on paper towels. Wipe pan out and return to stove, reducing heat to medium-high. Add 2 tablespoons olive oil to pot and then add chicken. Brown chicken for 2 to 3 minutes. Add fennel, onion, garlic, and bay leaf. Cover pot and cook vegetables for 5 to 6 minutes, stirring occasionally.

Remove cover and add beans, tomatoes, chicken broth, rosemary, thyme, and black pepper. Bring to a boil, reduce heat to low, and simmer until ready to serve. For a thinner soup, add up to 2 cups water.

Serve soup with chunks of garlic bread for dipping or float garlic croutons on top of the soup.

Chicken and Dumplin' Soup

SERVES 4 TO 6

1 pound boneless, skinless chicken (breasts,
  thighs, or a mixture)

A handful all-purpose flour

Coarse salt and black pepper, to taste

1 teaspoon Old Bay poultry seasoning
  (1/3 palmful)

2 tablespoons extra-virgin olive oil (once around
  the pan)

3 stalks celery from the heart, finely chopped

1 medium white onion, chopped

2 white potatoes, peeled and diced

3 carrots, peeled and diced

1 bay leaf, fresh or dried

1 box Jiffy biscuit mix, prepared following
  directions on box

A handful fresh flat-leaf parsley, chopped

2 quarts (32 ounces each) chicken broth

1/2 cup (a couple of handfuls) frozen green
  peas (optional)

Cut chicken into bite-size chunks. Spill a handful or two of flour onto a shallow dish. Add salt, pepper, and poultry seasoning to flour. Coat the chicken bits by tossing them all through the flour and rolling them around a bit. Discard the extra flour and wash hands.

Heat 2 tablespoons olive oil in a large, deep pot over medium-high heat. Place chicken pieces in hot oil and lightly brown, 3 or 4 minutes on each side. Add the chopped veggies and bay leaf, cover pot, and cook 5 minutes, stirring occasionally.

While veggies cook, mix up one box of Jiffy biscuit mix according to directions on the box, adding a handful of parsley to the batter.

Add chicken broth to pot. Bring broth to a boil. Drop in teaspoons of batter. Cover the pot tightly and simmer 8 minutes.

Uncover pot, add peas, and cook an additional minute. Adjust salt and pepper to taste.

Leftovers only get better—don't be afraid of making a whole batch of this soup even if you live alone.

Portuguese Sausage and Greens Soup

SERVES 4

2 tablespoons extra-virgin olive oil (twice
    around the pan)

3 medium white potatoes, peeled and diced

2 medium onions, peeled and chopped

4 to 6 cloves garlic, minced

2 bay leaves, fresh or dried

1 pound kale, mustard greens, or dandelion
    greens, washed, dried, and chopped

Coarse salt and black pepper, to taste

1 can (15 ounces) garbanzo beans (chickpeas)

1 can (15 ounces) diced tomatoes

3/4 pound andouille, chorizo, or linguiça sausage

1 quart (32 ounces) chicken broth

Warm, crusty bread

Heat olive oil in a deep pot over medium to medium-high heat. Add potatoes and onions, cover, and cook 5 minutes, stirring occasionally.

Add garlic, bay leaves, and kale or other greens and season with salt and pepper. Cover and cook until kale is wilted. Add beans, tomatoes, sausage, and broth and bring to a boil. Reduce heat to low and simmer 10 minutes, or until ready to serve.

Serve with hunks of garlic bread or crusty semolina bread for dunking.

Turkey Corn Chili

SERVES 4

Moms report that kids go for this chili, too.

1 medium onion, chopped
1 tablespoon corn or vegetable oil (1 turn
    around the pan)
2 cloves garlic, chopped
1 1/3 pounds ground lean turkey
1 small red bell pepper, seeded and chopped
1 1/2 cups frozen corn kernels
1 can (32 ounces) diced tomatoes
3 scallions, chopped
1 teaspoon poultry seasoning (1/3 palmful)
1 1/2 tablespoons chili powder (1/2 handful)
1 tablespoon ground cumin (1/3 handful)
1 to 2 ounces cayenne pepper sauce such as
    Red Hot or Tabasco, or to taste
Coarse salt and freshly ground black pepper,
    to taste
Shredded cheese and tortilla chips for topping
    and dipping

In a deep saucepot over medium high heat, sauté onion in oil for 3 to 5 minutes.

Add garlic and cook 1 minute more. Add turkey, browning for 5 minutes. Add bell pepper, corn, and tomatoes. Bring to a bubble, stirring in scallions, spices, cayenne pepper sauce, and salt and pepper.

Reduce heat and simmer 10 minutes.

Serve in bowls topped with cheese and chips on the side.

Claude's Creole Chili
SERVES 4

1 pound ground pork
1 tablespoon vegetable or corn oil (once around the pan)
1 medium onion, chopped
1 medium green bell pepper, seeded and chopped
2 stalks celery, chopped
1 bay leaf, fresh or dried
1 can (14 ounces) diced tomatoes
1 can (14 ounces) chicken broth
1 tablespoon ground cumin (half a palmful)
1 tablespoon chili powder (half a palmful)
6 drops cayenne pepper sauce, such as Red Hot or Tabasco
1/2 pound andouille or chorizo sausage, diced
Coarse salt, to taste
4 scallions, thinly sliced, to garnish

4 corn muffins, split and grilled or toasted

In a large, deep saucepot, brown pork in oil over medium-high heat, 3 to 5 minutes. Add onion, bell pepper, celery, and bay leaf. Cook until veggies are tender, 3 to 5 minutes more.

Add tomatoes and broth and heat through. Season with cumin, chili, and cayenne pepper sauce. Add sausage and heat through, another 2 or 3 minutes. Add salt if you feel it needs it.

Serve with a garnish of chopped scallions and warm, toasted corn muffins.

Manly Manny's Chili
MAKES 2 QUARTS, UP TO 6 BOWLFULS

My little brother Manny, now 20-something, can unload half the fridge into a pot and make the best-anything you've ever tasted. Smoky, spicy, and made of readily available ingredients, this chili is definitely a macho meal. It freezes well, too.

2 tablespoons corn or vegetable oil (twice around the pan)

1 large onion, chopped fine

4 cloves garlic, minced

1 1/2 pounds ground sirloin, 90% lean

Montreal Steak Seasoning or coarse salt and black pepper, to taste

1/2 bottle beer (6 ounces)

1 can (14 ounces) beef broth

1 can (6 ounces) tomato paste

1 1/2 tablespoons dark chili powder (a generous palmful)

1 tablespoon ground cumin (a little less than the chili powder)

2 ounces smoky barbecue sauce (2 glugs)

2 ounces Frank's Red Hot or other cayenne pepper sauce (about 3 tablespoons)

6 ounces shredded smoked cheddar cheese for topping (optional)

Chopped raw onions, for garnish (optional)

Corn tortilla chips, for dipping

Heat oil in a deep pot over medium-high heat. Add onions and garlic and sauté 3 to 5 minutes, stirring frequently, till onions are soft. Add ground beef and brown, another 3 to 5 minutes. Season meat and onions lightly with Montreal seasoning or salt and pepper. Add beer and let it reduce by half.

Stir in broth, paste, chili powder, cumin, smoky barbecue sauce and cayenne pepper sauce. Reduce heat to medium low and simmer 10 minutes.

Serve with shredded smoked cheddar cheese and chopped raw onions and corn chips.

Stovetop Macaroni and Smoked Cheddar Cheese

SERVES 6

1 pound elbow macaroni, cooked until al dente, about 8 minutes

1 medium onion, finely chopped

3 tablespoons butter

2 tablespoons vegetable oil

3 tablespoons flour (2 palmfuls)

1 1/2 cups, 1- or 2% milk

1/2 pound smoked cheddar cheese, shredded

1/4 to 1/3 pound Gruyère or Swiss cheese, shredded

Black pepper, to taste

2 or 3 pinches nutmeg (about 1/2 teaspoon)

4 to 6 dashes cayenne pepper sauce, such as Tabasco or Red Hot

3/4 cup plain bread crumbs (a couple of handfuls)

Cook macaroni, drain, and return to pot to keep warm.

In a deep saucepot over medium heat, sauté onion in 2 tablespoons of the butter and the oil for 5 minutes. Whisk in flour. Stirring frequently, cook mixture 3 to 5 minutes, until golden. While mixture cooks, heat milk in a glass container or measuring cup in microwave oven on high for 90 seconds or heat in a small pan on stove to simmer. Slowly whisk milk into onion mixture and combine until milk begins to thicken. Add cheeses and stir continuously until cheese is just melted.

Remove from heat and stir in black pepper and nutmeg. Cover and let stand.

In a small pan over medium heat, melt remaining 1 tablespoon butter and add several dashes of cayenne pepper sauce. Add bread crumbs and toast until golden, 2 or 3 minutes.

To assemble, add macaroni to sauce and coat it evenly. Scoop macaroni and cheese sauce into bowls and top with toasted bread crumbs. Serve with sautéed spinach or other dark greens and corn bread or toasted corn muffins.

Everything Jambalaya
SERVES 4

1 cup enriched white rice, following directions
    on package
1 tablespoon extra-virgin olive oil (once around
    the pan)
1 tablespoon butter
1 pound boneless, skinless chicken thighs or
    breast meat, diced
1/2 pound andouille, chorizo, or linguiça
    sausage, diced
1 medium onion, chopped
2 stalks celery from heart of stalk, chopped
1 green bell pepper, seeded and chopped
1 bay leaf, fresh or dried
A few drops cayenne pepper sauce
2 to 3 tablespoons all-purpose flour (a handful)
1 can (14 ounces) diced tomatoes
1 can (14 ounces) chicken broth
1 teaspoon ground cumin (1/4 palmful)
1 rounded teaspoon chili powder (1/4 palmful)
1 rounded teaspoon Old Bay seasoning
    (1/4 palmful)
4 drops each cayenne pepper sauce, such as
    Tabasco, and Worcestershire sauce
3/4 pound medium shrimp, peeled and deveined
Coarse salt and black pepper, to taste
4 sprigs fresh thyme leaves, stripped from stems
    and chopped (about 2 tablespoons)
4 scallions, sliced thin

Cook rice and keep covered.

Place a large, deep skillet over medium-high heat. Add oil to pan and melt butter into it. Add chicken and brown 2 minutes. Add sausage and cook 2 minutes more. Add onion, celery, bell pepper, bay leaf, and cayenne pepper sauce. Sauté veggies till tender, another 3 to 5 minutes. Sprinkle flour over vegetables and chicken and cook a minute more, stirring to incorporate flour. Add tomatoes and broth to pan and combine ingredients well. Season with cumin, chili powder, Old Bay seasoning, Tabasco, and Worcestershire.

Scatter shrimp into pot and cook until shrimp are pink and firm and sauce thickens a bit, about 3 minutes. Season with salt and pepper to taste.

To serve, ladle jambalaya into bowls. Scoop rice with an ice cream scoop and place 1 scoop in the center of each dish of jambalaya. Top rice and jambalaya with chopped thyme and scallions.

Red Beans and Rice
SERVES 4

This dish is traditionally made with a ham bone or ham hocks. I prefer hot smoked sausage and ham.

2 cups water
1 cup enriched white rice

1 can (15 ounces) red kidney beans
1 tablespoon vegetable oil (once around the pan)
1 tablespoon butter
1/2 pound andouille, chorizo, or linguiça
    sausage, diced
1/2 pound smoked ham, diced
1 medium onion, chopped
1 stalk celery, diced
2 cloves garlic, minced
1 bay leaf, fresh or dried
1 cup chicken broth, or half a 12-ounce bottle
    of beer
2 teaspoons ground cumin (1/3 palmful)
1 teaspoon sweet paprika (1/4 palmful)
5 or 6 drops cayenne pepper sauce, such as
    Tabasco or Red Hot
5 or 6 drops Worcestershire sauce
Coarse salt and black pepper, to taste
4 scallions, thinly sliced

Place a small saucepan with the 2 cups water on the stove and bring water to a boil. Add rice and bring water back to a boil. Reduce heat to low, cover pot, and simmer 20 minutes, or until tender. Remove from heat and let stand.

While rice cooks, prepare meat and vegetables. Drain and rinse beans and set aside. Place a deep skillet or heavy-bottomed pot over medium-high heat. Add oil and butter. Sauté meat bits 2 minutes, stirring frequently. Add onion, celery, garlic, and bay leaf. Cook vegetables 5 minutes, stirring frequently.

Deglaze pan by adding chicken broth or beer—scrape up all the good stuff from the bottom of the pot. Add red beans. Allow liquid to reduce by half.

Add cumin, paprika, cayenne pepper sauce, and Worcestershire. Add cooked rice to pot and coat evenly with pan juices. Season to taste with salt and pepper and top with chopped scallions.

Chicken and Orzo

SERVES 4

2 tablespoons extra-virgin olive oil (twice
    around the pan)

1 small onion, chopped fine

2 small cloves garlic, peeled and chopped fine

3 or 4 sprigs fresh thyme, stripped from stems
    and chopped, or 1/2 teaspoon (a few
    pinches) dried thyme

2 cans (14 1/2 ounces each) chicken broth

2 cups orzo pasta

1 pound chicken tenders or boneless, skinless
    chicken breast, diced

1/2 cup grated Romano or Parmigiano cheese
    (a handful)

Freshly ground black pepper, to taste

In a deep skillet, heat olive oil over medium heat, add onion and garlic, and cook 2 to 3 minutes. Add thyme and broth and bring to a boil. Add orzo and chicken and stir. Reduce heat to a simmer and cover. Cook until liquid is absorbed, about 20 minutes.

Stir in cheese and black pepper and serve immediately.

A spinach salad or baby mixed green salad and warm crusty bread round out this meal nicely.

Burgers and Sandwiches

There are times when nothing will satisfy
except a big, juicy burger made of the freshest
ingredients, and grilled to perfection just
before eating. Am I right?

If the idea of a smoky Barbecued Beef Burger
doesn't turn you on, try the Portobello Burger
with Spinach Pesto and Smoked Cheese, a
dish so flavorful that it will inspire you to
"go vegetarian" on the spot.

American All-Star Burgers

MAKES 4 BURGERS

1 pound ground sirloin (93% lean)

1/2 small onion, chopped fine

2 tablespoons sweet pickle relish

6 drops cayenne pepper sauce, such as Red Hot
    or Tabasco

Montreal Steak Seasoning by McCormick, or
    coarse salt and black pepper, to taste

BASTING SAUCE

1/4 cup ketchup

1/4 cup steak sauce

4 crusty rolls, split

Leaf lettuce, sliced tomato, and sliced red
    onion, for topping

Combine meat, onion, relish, cayenne pepper sauce, and seasoning. Form into 4 patties. Grill on griddle pan or in a nonstick skillet 6 minutes, then flip.

Combine ketchup and steak sauce and baste burgers with sauce; cook 4 or 5 minutes longer. Use same method for outdoor grilling.

Place on rolls and top with lettuce and sliced tomato and red onion.

Meatball Burgers

MAKES 6 BURGERS

1/2 pound ground sirloin
1/2 pound ground pork
1 large egg, beaten
1 large clove garlic, minced
1/2 cup Italian bread crumbs (2 handfuls)
1/4 cup grated cheese (a handful)
A handful chopped fresh flat-leaf parsley
2 pinches crushed red pepper flakes
3 pinches dried oregano
Ground black pepper, to taste
1 can (14 ounces) pizza sauce
4 crusty rolls, split and toasted
8 ounces shredded mozzarella or provolone
    cheese

Combine meats with egg, garlic, bread crumbs, grated cheese, parsley, red pepper flakes, oregano, and black pepper. Form into patties.

Preheat large nonstick skillet over medium-high heat. Cook patties 6 to 8 minutes on each side and remove from pan. Add pizza sauce and heat. Add patties back to pan and cook in sauce a minute more.

Pile burgers on crusty rolls and top with a pile of shredded cheese.

Barbecued Beef Burgers

MAKES 4 BURGERS

1 1/2 teaspoons butter (a pat)
1 small cooking or boiling onion, chopped fine
1 pound ground sirloin
1/3 cup smoky barbecue sauce (a couple of glugs)
Montreal Steak Seasoning by McCormick,
    to taste
6 ounces smoked cheddar cheese, grated
4 crusty rolls, split
4 leaves red or green leaf lettuce
Sliced tomato
Thin-sliced red onion

Melt butter in a small skillet over medium heat. Add onion and cook 5 or 6 minutes, till tender. Remove from heat and let cool.

Place beef in a bowl and combine with barbecue sauce and cooked onion. Form into 4 patties and season with Montreal Steak Seasoning.

Heat a grill pan over medium-high heat. Cook patties 6 minutes on each side. Pile cheese on top of each burger and remove pan from heat. Cover loosely with aluminum foil to melt cheese. Pile burgers on buns and top with lettuce, tomato, and red onion.

Chicken Club Sandwiches

MAKES 4 SANDWICHES

4 pieces boneless, skinless chicken breast,
4 to 6 ounces each
Coarse salt and black pepper, to taste
Juice of 1/2 lemon
1 tablespoon extra-virgin olive oil
6 drops cayenne pepper sauce, such as Tabasco
1/2 teaspoon poultry seasoning
A large plastic food storage bag
4 crusty rolls, split
8 slices bacon, cooked until crisp under broiler
or in microwave
Lettuce and sliced tomatoes, for topping
1/2 cup prepared ranch dressing

Season chicken with salt and pepper. Pour lemon juice, oil, cayenne pepper sauce, and poultry seasoning into a food storage bag. Place chicken in bag and coat evenly with marinade.

Heat a grill pan or skillet over medium-high heat. Cook chicken 6 minutes on each side and remove from heat. Let stand 5 minutes. Slice breasts on an angle.

To assemble, pile chicken on a roll bottom and top with crisp bacon, lettuce, and tomato. Spread bun tops with 2 tablespoons ranch dressing and replace roll tops.

World-Class Tuna Melt
MAKES 4 MELTS

4 sandwich-size sourdough English muffins, split

2 cans (6 ounces each) chunk Albacore tuna, drained and flaked

3 canned whole artichoke hearts, packed in water, drained and chopped

1 teaspoon Old Bay seasoning (1/3 palmful)

1/4 small red onion, chopped fine

12 Kalamata olives, pitted and chopped

Zest of 1 lemon

2 tablespoons mayonnaise

Coarse salt and black pepper, to taste

4 ounces Gruyère or Emmentaler Swiss, sliced thin

Toast English muffins.

Combine all other ingredients except cheese. Pile tuna on 4 half muffins and top with cheese. Place under hot broiler and melt. Replace muffin tops and serve with slaw salad, homemade or storebought.

Crab Melts

MAKES 4 OPEN-FACE MELTS

CRAB SALAD

12 ounces lump canned crabmeat, drained

3 stalks celery from heart of stalk, chopped fine

2 hard-boiled eggs, chopped

1 roasted red pepper or pimiento, chopped

1 teaspoon Old Bay seasoning (1/3 palmful)

12 blades fresh chives, chopped

Juice of 1/2 lemon

Coarse salt and black pepper, to taste

1/4 cup mayonnaise

MELT FIXINS:

1 small avocado, pitted, peeled, sliced, and
    coated with a little lemon juice

1 medium vine-ripe tomato, sliced

4 slices Swiss cheese

4 lettuce leaves, red or green leaf

2 sandwich-size English muffins, split and
    toasted

Combine all Crab Salad ingredients in a bowl.

Arrange avocado and tomato slices on English muffin halves. Pile crab salad on top of tomatoes and avocados. Cover with cheese and melt under broiler. Place a lettuce leaf on each half and top with remaining English muffin halves.

Antipasto Grinder

MAKES 4 SANDWICHES

1 baguette (loaf of long, crusty bread)

1 clove garlic, crushed

3 tablespoons extra-virgin olive oil

2 cans (6 ounces each) Albacore tuna, drained

1/2 small red onion, sliced thin

4 ounces hot peppers, pepperoncini or banana peppers, chopped

1 can (14 ounces) artichoke hearts, packed in water, drained and chopped

1 bottle (16 ounces) roasted red peppers, drained

3 ounces capers, drained and rinsed

20 Kalamata olives, pitted and chopped

A few grinds black pepper

6 ounces sliced sharp provolone cheese

Cut baguette in half lengthwise and hollow out the middle.

Cover garlic with oil in a small dish and microwave on high for 30 seconds or heat garlic and oil in small pan over medium heat until garlic speaks or sizzles. Brush bread evenly with oil.

Stuff bread halves with remaining ingredients, packing them down in layers. Place one half baguette on top of the other and cut stuffed loaf into 4 sandwiches.

Portobello Burgers with Spinach Pesto and Smoked Cheese

MAKES 4 "BURGERS"

SPINACH PESTO

5 ounces triple-washed baby spinach leaves
(half a sack)

2 ounces walnut pieces (2 handfuls), toasted in
toaster oven or small skillet

1 clove garlic, crushed

2 tablespoons extra-virgin olive oil (twice
around the pan)

2 pinches ground nutmeg

Coarse salt and black pepper, to taste

2 ounces grated Romano or Parmigiano
cheese (a handful)

PORTOBELLO CAPS

4 medium portobello mushroom caps

1 large plastic food storage bag

2 tablespoons extra-virgin olive oil (twice
around the pan)

2 tablespoons Worcestershire sauce (10 to
12 drops)

1 tablespoon balsamic vinegar (a small splash)

2 sprigs fresh rosemary, stripped from stems and
chopped fine

Montreal Steak Seasoning by McCormick, or
coarse salt and black pepper, to taste

FIXINS

1/2 pound smoked fresh mozzarella, sliced thin

4 large round crusty rolls, split

1/2 small red onion, sliced thin

Remaining baby spinach greens (5 ounces)

For Spinach Pesto, place the half-sack baby spinach in a food processor with the walnuts. Place the clove of garlic in a small dish and cover with the 2 tablespoons extra-virgin oil. Microwave on high for 30 seconds. Or, heat garlic and oil in a small pan over medium heat until garlic speaks or sizzles. Let oil stand 2 minutes, then add to spinach and nuts. Add the nutmeg, a little salt and pepper, and the handful of cheese to processor and pulse into a paste.

Brush portobello caps with a damp towel to clean them. In a large food storage bag, combine olive oil, Worcestershire, balsamic vinegar, and rosemary. Add caps and coat. Heat a grill pan or large nonstick skillet over medium-high heat. Place caps on hot grill and season lightly with Montreal seasoning or salt and pepper. Grill 5 minutes, top side up, then 3 minutes cap side down. Top with smoked mozzarella. Remove pan from heat and cover loosely with aluminum foil tent and let stand 3 minutes.

To serve, place cap on roll bottom. Spread roll top with pesto. Top mushroom caps with red onion and spinach leaves and replace roll top.

Sausage Sandwiches
SERVES 4

This is the most delicious sausage sandwich in the world. Make it and know for yourself.

4 sweet Italian sausage patties (1/4 pound each)

12 ounces giardiniera (hot pickled vegetable salad), drained (see Note)

A handful fresh flat-leaf parsley

1 beefsteak tomato, halved, seeded, and sliced thin

1/2 red onion, sliced very thin

Extra-virgin olive oil (a good drizzle)

Red wine vinegar (a splash)

Pinch of coarse salt

Black pepper, to taste

4 leaves green- or red-leaf lettuce

4 crusty rolls, split

Heat a grill pan or skillet over medium-high heat. Place patties on hot pan and cook 6 minutes on each side. Patties may also be cooked over outdoor grill 6 inches from heat for the same cooking time.

Combine giardiniera salad and parsley leaves in a food processor. Pulse into a fine relish.

Toss sliced tomatoes and onions with a little oil and vinegar and season with salt and pepper.

To assemble, coat bottom of roll with chopped relish and top with sausage, tomato and onion slices, lettuce leaf, and roll top. Serve with a chunky vegetable salad and oven fries or root-vegetable chips.

Note: Giardiniera is Italian pickled cauliflower, carrots, and peppers in brine. It is available in the Italian foods section of your local market.

Spicy Turkey Burgers

MAKES 6 BURGERS

1 1/3 pounds ground turkey breast
1 tablespoon ground cumin (half a palmful)
1/4 teaspoon ground cinnamon (2 or 3 pinches)
Coarse salt and black pepper, to taste
Zest of 1 lemon
3 scallions, sliced thin
A handful currants
1/2 small onion, chopped fine
1/3 cup ketchup

1 teaspoon vegetable or extra-virgin olive oil
6 Kaiser rolls, split
Tahini sesame sauce, prepared, or ranch
      dressing, to spread on buns
Lettuce leaves
Tomato and red onion, sliced thin

Combine first 9 ingredients and form into 6 patties. Grill over medium-high heat in a non-stick skillet in a touch of oil for 6 minutes on each side.

Pile burgers on buns spread with tahini sauce or ranch dressing and top with lettuce, tomato, and onion.

New England Turkey Burgers with Cranberry Sauce

MAKES 4 LARGE BURGERS

1 1/4 pounds (1 package) 93% to 99% fat-free ground turkey

1/2 small onion, finely chopped

1/2 stalk celery from heart of stalk, finely chopped

A handful fresh parsley, finely chopped, or 1 teaspoon dried parsley flakes

1 teaspoon poultry seasoning (1/4 palmful)

Coarse salt and black pepper, to taste

1 tablespoon vegetable or extra-virgin olive oil (once around the pan)

4 sandwich-size English muffins, toasted

1 can (15 ounces) whole berry cranberry sauce

1 head Bibb lettuce, washed and dried

Place turkey in a bowl and combine with onion, celery, parsley, poultry seasoning, and salt and pepper. Combine well and form into 4 large patties.

Heat oil in nonstick skillet over medium-high heat. Cook burgers 5 minutes on each side.

To assemble, pile burgers on muffin bottoms and top with cranberry relish, Bibb lettuce, and muffin tops. Serve with prepared frozen veggies like butternut squash or corn on the cob, or garnish your plate with a serving of fresh fruit such as grapes and sliced apples or pears.

Chicken

A friend of mine says, "Chicken Fricassee was popular when I was" (some 30 years ago), yet it remains a delicious comfort food. Best served with warm biscuits and cold milk, this retro dish is a soothing, creamy delight.

Quick Chicken Croquettes and Tuscan Style Chicken Cutlets and Creamy Spinach are top hits, too. Even with the kids!

Chicken Fricassee

SERVES 4

Mom, it's not yours, but it's close.

1 to 1 1/3 pounds boneless, skinless chicken breast (four 4- to 5-ounce breast halves)

1/2 teaspoon poultry seasoning (a few good pinches)

A few pinches coarse salt and a few grinds of black pepper

1 tablespoon extra-virgin olive oil (once around the pan, plus a drizzle more)

1 tablespoon butter

2 medium carrots, peeled, and chopped fine

4 scallions, chopped

1 large shallot, chopped fine

1/2 cup dry white wine (or add an extra 1/2 cup chicken broth instead)

1 cup chicken broth

3 or 4 sprigs fresh tarragon, very thinly sliced (about 2 tablespoons)

2 to 3 tablespoons superfine flour, such as Wondra brand

4 prepared buttermilk biscuits (available in many bakery departments), or 1 package (6.9 ounces) rice pilaf, such as Near East brand, cooked following directions on box

Season chicken with poultry seasoning and salt and pepper. Lightly brown chicken in the tablespoon of olive oil, 2 or 3 minutes per side, over medium to medium-high heat in a large non-stick skillet. Remove chicken and set aside.

Add a little more oil and butter to pan. Add veggies and sauté 5 minutes. Add wine or broth and allow it to reduce by half, 1 or 2 more minutes.

Add chicken back to pan and pour in broth. Cook chicken 5 or 6 minutes more, until meat is tender yet cooked through. Stir in tarragon.

Combine superfine flour with a splash of broth or water and stir into a thin paste. Add paste to pan and combine with juices using a whisk. Thicken to desired consistency (1 or 2 minutes should do it). Adjust seasonings to taste with salt and pepper.

Serve over split biscuits or prepared rice pilaf.

Creole Chicken Breasts
with Crab and Artichoke Stuffing

SERVES 4

For my dad, James Claude.

1 to 1 1/2 pounds chicken breast cutlets, pounded thin
Coarse salt and black pepper, to taste
A few pinches poultry seasoning

CRAB AND ARTICHOKE STUFFING

2 shallots, chopped fine
1 stalk celery from the heart, chopped fine
2 tablespoons extra-virgin olive oil (twice around the pan)
1 can (14 ounces) artichoke hearts in water, drained and chopped
1/2 cup chicken broth (3 or 4 splashes)
8 to 10 ounces canned crabmeat
2 slices white bread, toasted and buttered
1 teaspoon Old Bay seasoning (1/4 palmful)
Coarse salt and black pepper, to taste

CREOLE SAUCE

1 tablespoon extra-virgin olive oil (once around the pan)
1 pat butter (about 1/2 tablespoon)
1 cup dry sherry
1 cup chicken broth
1 tablespoons cornstarch dissolved in a splash of water or broth

Season cutlets with salt, pepper, and poultry seasoning. Set aside.

For stuffing, in a skillet over medium heat, sauté shallots and celery in olive oil for 2 or 3 minutes. Add artichoke hearts and 1/2 cup broth; cook a minute more. Add crabmeat and heat through, breaking up meat. Cube toast into small dice and add to pan. Season with Old Bay seasoning, salt, and pepper and combine ingredients until bread is moist. Remove from heat.

Place small mounds of stuffing on cutlets and roll up. Secure breasts with toothpicks.

For sauce, heat a nonstick skillet over medium-high heat. Add oil and butter to pan. Place breasts in pan and brown 2 or 3 minutes on each side. Remove chicken. Add sherry and reduce by half, cooking 1 or 2 minutes. Add broth and bring to a boil. Add cornstarch and thicken sauce. Return chicken to pan. Cover and simmer 5 minutes, or until chicken is cooked through.

Serve chicken with a green salad and crusty French bread.

The Ultimate Chicken Cutlets
SERVES 4

This may be my recipe, but no one makes them better than my sweetheart, Rick.

1 to 1 1/2 pounds boneless, skinless chicken
   breasts
Large plastic food storage bags
1/2 cup all-purpose flour
3 large eggs or 1 cup egg substitute
1 1/2 cups plain bread crumbs
3 sprigs fresh rosemary, chopped very fine
   (about 2 tablespoons)
6 sprigs fresh thyme leaves, chopped fine (about
   2 tablespoons)
A handful fresh flat-leaf parsley, chopped fine
1/2 to 2/3 cup grated Parmigiano cheese
   (a couple handfuls)
2 pinches coarse salt
Freshly ground black pepper, to taste
3 to 4 tablespoons extra-virgin olive oil (3 or 4
   turns of the pan), total
3 or 4 pats of butter (about 1/2 tablespoon
   each) 1 1/2 tablespoons total
1 recipe 15-Minute Marinara (recipe follows), or
   1 quart jarred sauce

Preheat oven to 300 degrees F and place a
cookie sheet on the center rack of oven.

Butterfly each piece of chicken breast by cutting
into 2 thin fillets. Place 2 fillets at a time in a large
food storage bag a few inches apart. Pound
breasts with a meat mallet until very thin.
Remove cutlets from bag and repeat with remaining
cutlets. One pound of meat should yield 8
cutlets. Place flour in a shallow dish. Beat eggs or
egg substitute with a splash of water and pour
into a shallow bowl. Set bowl next to flour dish.
In a third shallow bowl or platter, combine bread
crumbs, herbs, cheese, and salt and pepper.

Heat a large skillet over medium heat. Add 2
tablespoons extra-virgin oil (twice around the
pan) and 1 pat butter. When butter has melted
into oil, begin coating cutlets in flour, then
egg, then bread crumbs and adding coated
slices to pan. Cook cutlets in batches in single
layers, adding a little more oil and another pat
of butter to pan with each batch. Brown cutlets
3 minutes or so on each side, till golden, then
transfer to cookie sheet in oven to finish cooking,
2 or 3 minutes more.

Top cutlets with a little marinara sauce and serve
with crusty semolina bread and a green salad.

Variation

For cheesier cutlets, layer sauce and 1/2 pound sliced fresh mozzarella or smoked mozzarella, Asiago, or provolone cheese over chicken. Place chicken under the broiler on high until cheese begins to brown at edges.

A side of fresh pasta tossed with a little extra marinara sauce makes this meal even heartier—*abbundanza*.

15-Minute Marinara

2 to 3 tablespoons extra-virgin olive oil (2 or 3 turns around the pan)

4 large cloves garlic, chopped fine

2 or 3 pinches crushed red pepper flakes

1 can (28 ounces) whole tomatoes, seeded and coarsely chopped

1 can (28 ounces) crushed tomatoes

2 sprigs fresh oregano, chopped fine (about 1 tablespoon)

A handful fresh flat-leaf parsley, chopped fine

12 to 15 leaves fresh basil, stacked one atop another, rolled into a log then sliced thin

Coarse salt and black pepper, to taste

Place a deep skillet over medium to medium-low heat. Add oil and garlic and crushed red pepper flakes. Let garlic begin to speak by sizzling in oil; stir frequently to keep garlic from browning and turning bitter. Add whole tomatoes and crushed tomatoes. Stir in herbs and salt and pepper and let sauce come to a boil. Reduce heat and simmer 10 minutes, or until ready to serve.

Parmesan-Crusted Chicken with Tomato and Onion Relish

SERVES 4

1 to 1 1/4 pounds boneless, skinless chicken breasts

2 cups shredded (*not* grated) Parmesan cheese
(1 tub from fancy cheese section of market,
such as DiGiorno brand)

Several grinds coarse black pepper

1 tablespoon extra-virgin olive oil (once around
the pan)

TOMATO AND ONION RELISH

5 plum tomatoes, seeded and diced

1 small cooking or boiling onion, chopped fine

A handful fresh flat-leaf parsley

A few pinches coarse salt, to taste

A slight drizzle extra-virgin olive oil

Trim chicken of any excess fat or skin. Place shredded Parmigiano seasoned with black pepper on a shallow dish or plate. Press each side of each chicken breast into cheese. Set coated chicken aside.

Place a large, nonstick skillet over medium-high heat. Add olive oil, then chicken. Cook chicken about 6 to 8 minutes on each side, until cheese is golden brown and crisp and juices from breast run clear when pierced. Do not turn chicken before first side is golden brown in color. Remove breasts from heat and let stand for 1 or 2 minutes so meat juices can redistribute.

Combine all ingredients for relish in a bowl and toss. Serve chicken with a generous pile of relish and a tossed green salad; oven fries or onion and garlic or other specialty chips round out the meal.

Variation

Coat chicken tenders (rather than breasts) with cheese and follow same method. Omit topping and serve with warm pizza sauce for dipping.

Cacciatore Pasta Toss

SERVES UP TO 4

1 tablespoon extra-virgin olive oil (once around
    the pan)

2 or 3 pinches crushed red pepper flakes

1 pound boneless, skinless chicken breast or
    tenderloins, cut into bite-size chunks

4 to 6 cloves garlic, cracked or coarsely
    chopped

1 tablespoons extra-virgin oil (once around
    the pan)

2 portobello mushrooms, or 8 crimini
    mushrooms, thinly sliced, then chopped

1 medium onion, chopped

1 red or green bell pepper, seeded and chopped

6 to 7 ounces (half a can) beef or vegetable
    broth

1 can (15 ounces) crushed tomatoes

Black pepper, to taste

A handful chopped fresh flat-leaf parsley

1/2 pound rigatoni, cooked until al dente

Grated Parmigiano, Romano, or Asiago cheese,
    for topping

Crusty bread, for the table

Place a large nonstick skillet over medium-high heat. Add 1 tablespoon oil, red pepper flakes, chicken, and cracked or chopped garlic. Brown chicken, stirring frequently. Remove browned chicken from skillet and transfer to a platter.

Return pan to stove and add 1 tablespoon olive oil and the mushrooms. Cover pan and reduce heat to medium. Cook mushrooms until dark and tender. Add onion and red or green pepper. Cover and cook 1 or 2 more minutes. Add broth and tomatoes and season sauce with black pepper.

Return chicken to the pan and combine cacciatore with parsley and cooked, drained pasta. Serve with freshly grated cheese and warm bread

Chicken with Roasted Red Peppers and Herb Cheese

SERVES 2 TO 3

1 pound chicken breast cutlets

1 large plastic food storage bag

8 ounces garlic-and-herb soft cheese, such as Alouette brand

2 scallions, sliced thin, on an angle

12 ounces roasted red peppers, drained and patted dry

Toothpicks

2 tablespoons extra-virgin olive oil (twice around the pan)

Coarse salt and black pepper to taste

Place chicken breasts, 2 at a time, in a large plastic food storage bag. Pound breasts to 1/8-inch thickness and remove. Repeat with remaining chicken.

Spread each breast cutlet with a thin layer of cheese and sprinkle with sliced scallions. Place a roasted pepper on top of each cutlet. Roll breasts into bundles and secure with toothpicks.

Place a large, nonstick skillet over medium-high heat. When the pan is hot, add oil and bundles. Brown and cook chicken breasts 6 minutes on each side. Season with salt and pepper. Remove breasts and slice. Fan out the breasts and serve with a chunky vegetable or green salad and crusty bread.

Cordon Bleu Roll-Ups

SERVES 4

1 pound chicken breast cutlets

1 large plastic food storage bag

1/4 pound thin-sliced prosciutto (Italian ham)

8 ounces fontina cheese, sliced thin

Toothpicks

2 handfuls all-purpose flour

Coarse salt and black pepper, to taste

A couple pinches poultry seasoning

2 tablespoons extra-virgin olive oil

2 pats butter (about 3 teaspoons), divided
    in half

1/2 cup dry white wine

1 cup chicken broth

2 tablespoons superfine flour, such as Wondra
    brand, dissolved in a splash of broth

A few sprigs fresh thyme leaves, chopped, to
    garnish

Place cutlets, 2 at a time, inside a large food storage bag and pound thin. Repeat until all cutlets are 1/8 inch thick. Place a slice of ham and a thin layer of cheese on each cutlet; roll cutlets into bundles and secure with toothpicks. Place flour on a platter and season with salt, pepper, and poultry seasoning.

Place a large nonstick skillet over medium-high heat. Add olive oil and half the butter. When butter melts into oil, place bundles in pan and cook 5 minutes on each side, until golden. Remove chicken from pan and add remaining butter and wine. Scrape up pan drippings with whisk. Reduce wine by half. Add broth and bring to a simmer. Whisk in superfine flour paste and thicken sauce 1 or 2 minutes. Add bundles back to pan, reduce heat, cover, and simmer a last minute or two.

To serve, remove bundles and pull out toothpicks. Slice on an angle and fan out chicken. Top with a drizzle of sauce and sprinkle with thyme leaves. Crusty bread and a salad round out your meal.

Quick Chicken Croquettes

MAKES 10 2-INCH PATTIES

This croquette recipe will make patties, instead of cones, for easy pan frying.

CHICKEN PATTIES

2 packages (5 to 6 ounces each) prepared sliced
 grilled chicken breast, such as Purdue brand
1 cup prepared instant mashed potatoes, plain
 or chive flavor
1/2 cup plain bread crumbs, divided into
 equal amounts
1 teaspoon poultry seasoning (1/3 palmful)
1/4 teaspoon nutmeg (a few pinches)
Coarse salt and black pepper, to taste
1 large egg, beaten
1 stalk celery, chopped fine
1 small boiling onion, chopped very fine
4 baby carrots (from bulk bin of produce
 section), chopped fine
A handful chopped fresh flat-leaf parsley or
 1 tablespoon dried (a palmful)
1/4 cup all-purpose flour (a couple handfuls)
Canola oil, for frying

GRAVY

2 tablespoons butter
2 tablespoons all-purpose flour
1 can (14 ounces) chicken broth
Black pepper, to taste

Using a fork, shred chicken in a bowl. Add prepared potatoes, half of the bread crumbs, poultry seasoning, nutmeg, salt and pepper, egg, celery, onion, carrot, and parsley. Mix well and form 10 patties.

Heat 1/2-inch layer of oil in a deep, large skillet over medium-high heat.

Combine remaining bread crumbs and flour in a shallow dish. Coat patties and fry in a single layer in 2 batches for 4 to 5 minutes on each side or until deep golden. Drain on paper towels.

While second batch of patties is frying, melt butter in a small pan over medium-high heat until butter bubbles. Add flour and whisk 2 minutes. Add broth in a steady stream, whisking into butter and flour. Bring broth to a boil, then simmer 5 minutes, stirring occasionally with whisk, until desired thickness (gravy should coat back of spoon with a thin layer). Season with a little pepper to taste. Spoon gravy over patties. Yummy!

Serve with whole berry cranberry sauce, mashed potatoes, instant or homemade, and a tossed green salad.

Tuscan-Style Chicken Cutlets with Creamy Spinach

SERVES 4

1 1/3 to 1 1/2 pounds chicken breast cutlets

2 large plastic food storage bags

3 large eggs, beaten

1 cup all-purpose flour

1 teaspoon poultry seasoning (1/4 palmful)

Coarse salt and black pepper, to taste

Vegetable or extra-virgin olive oil, for frying

1 large lemon, cut into wedges

1 recipe Creamy Spinach (recipe follows)

Place cutlets in large food storage bags a few inches apart and lightly pound to 1/4-inch thickness.

Beat eggs in a shallow dish. Mix flour, poultry seasoning, and salt and pepper in a second dish.

Place a cookie sheet in oven on low heat, about 275 degrees F.

Heat 1/2 inch oil in a large, deep skillet over medium heat.

Coat chicken in flour, shaking off excess. Remove pieces one at a time. Coat each cutlet in egg, draining off excess. Add cutlets to oil, 2 or 3 at a time, and brown till lightly golden, 3 minutes on each side. Place cutlets in oven on low and repeat process until all the cutlets are done. Serve with lemon wedges and Creamy Spinach.

Creamy Spinach

1 1/2 bags (16 ounces) triple washed spinach

1 tablespoon extra-virgin olive oil (once around the pan)

1 pat butter (about 1 1/2 teaspoons)

1 medium shallot, peeled and chopped fine

1 1/2 tablespoons all-purpose flour (a generous sprinkle)

1 cup reduced-fat milk

3 ounces reduced-fat cream cheese (a little less than a half brick), softened

2 or 3 pinches nutmeg (1/4 teaspoon)

Coarse salt and black pepper, to taste

Sort spinach leaves and remove large, tough stems. Coarsely chop and set aside.

Heat a deep skillet over medium to medium low heat. Add oil and butter. When butter melts, add shallot and sauté for 2 or 3 minutes. Whisk in flour and cook a minute more. Add milk and whisk until smooth. Add cream cheese and whisk until melted. Add nutmeg. Place spinach into the pan in stages. Turn spinach in sauce, and as it wilts, add more and more greens. Season with salt and pepper.

Pork, Beef, and Lamb

When asked about favorite comfort foods, audiences invariably mention meatloaf and mashed potatoes. And I can understand why. When I eat meatloaf I'm a kid again, safe and satisfied. I'm home.

Memories of favorite childhood foods remain with us, and they influence our choice of comfort foods. A peanut butter and jelly sandwich anyone? Or how about a steaming plate of Swedish Meatballs and Egg Noodles?

Pork Schnitzel

SERVES 4

This recipe is one of many given to me by a fan. I'm ready to swap anytime!

4 thin-cut boneless pork loin chops
1 large plastic food storage bag
2 cups cracker meal (available in most markets
    near bread crumbs)
Coarse salt and black pepper, to taste
2 large eggs, beaten
1/4 cup milk or reduced-fat milk (2 splashes)
2 tablespoons extra-virgin olive oil (twice
    around the pan)
1 pat butter (about 1 1/2 teaspoons)
Grated fresh nutmeg, or a few pinches ground
1 lemon, cut into wedges

Place cutlets, 1 at a time, in a large plastic food storage bag. Pound cutlets with a meat mallet to 1/8 inch thickness. Pour cracker meal into a shallow dish and season with a little salt and pepper. Coat each pork cutlet in crumbs, shaking off excess. Combine eggs and milk in a second shallow dish. Dip each cutlet into egg, then turn a second time in cracker crumbs.

Heat a large, nonstick skillet over medium-high heat. Add 1 tablespoon olive oil (once around the pan), and half a pat of butter. Cook cutlets 2 at a time for 3 to 5 minutes on each side, until golden and crisp. Wipe pan clean, return to heat and repeat. Top cooked schnitzel with grated nutmeg or a sprinkling of ground nutmeg and serve with wedges of lemon.

Potato salad or potato pancakes with applesauce make a nice side dish.

Pork Chops and Applesauce
SERVES 6

6 boneless pork loin chops, 3/4 inch thick

Balsamic vinegar

1 tablespoon extra-virgin olive oil (once around the pan)

Black pepper

6 sprigs fresh thyme, chopped

2 feet aluminum foil, folded in half, then in half again

8 Macintosh apples, peeled, cored, and cut into chunks

1 cup (a small bottleful) all-natural apple juice

A couple pinches ground cinnamon

A palmful brown sugar

A pinch ground nutmeg

Rub chops with a little balsamic vinegar to flavor. Heat oil in a deep skillet over medium-high flame. Chops should sizzle when placed in pan. Cook chops 6 minutes. Turn. Season with pepper and thyme. Place an aluminum foil tent on top of the chops and cook another 6 minutes.

While chops cook, start cooking apple chunks and apple juice over medium-high heat. As the juice boils, stir and press the apples a bit as they cook down. (You want to leave the sauce chunky when you use nice fresh apples.) Sprinkle the sauce with cinnamon, sugar, and nutmeg. Reduce heat and simmer until sauce thickens, about 8 to 10 minutes.

Serve with spinach or salad of dark greens.

Hungarian Paprikas with Pork

SERVES 4

3 tablespoons all-purpose, unbleached flour
(a couple of handfuls)

1 1/2 tablespoons Hungarian sweet paprika
(half a palmful)

A few sprigs fresh marjoram, chopped, or
1 teaspoon dried

1 pound boneless pork loin chops, cut into
bite-size cubes

1/4 cup extra-virgin olive oil (3 or 4 turns around
the pan in a slow stream)

4 ounces drained, roasted red bell peppers
(1 small jar, or 1 whole homemade roasted
pepper)

1 can (28 ounces) stewed or diced tomatoes,
with celery, pepper and onion

1/2 cup sour cream, or reduced-fat sour cream

Salt and pepper, to taste

1 package (12 to 16 ounces) egg or semolina
fettuccini, or egg noodles, cooked until
al dente

2 tablespoons butter to coat noodles (optional)

A handful chopped fresh parsley, for noodles
(optional)

Combine flour, paprika, and marjoram in a shallow dish. Coat pork cubes in mixture.

Preheat deep skillet over medium-high heat. Add oil and allow it to heat for 30 seconds. Add meat cubes and cook 3 minutes on each side, giving the pan a good shake occasionally. Dice drained, jarred roasted red peppers or 1 whole homemade pepper. Add peppers and tomatoes to pan and stir up any pan drippings with a wooden spoon. Add sour cream and stir until combined; season with salt and pepper to taste.

Serve with buttered noodles sprinkled with parsley or over plain cooked egg or semolina pasta; add a green salad and some garlic toast for a well-rounded meal.

Pasta with Pumpkin and Sausage

SERVES 4 AS ENTRÉE, 8 AS AN APPETIZER

This dish is a fall favorite of my family.

2 drizzles extra-virgin olive oil

1 pound bulk sweet sausage

1 medium onion, chopped fine

4 cloves garlic, minced

1 bay leaf, fresh or dried

4 to 6 leaves fresh sage, slivered (about 1 1/2 tablespoons)

1 cup dry white wine

1 can (14 ounces) chicken broth

1 cup canned pumpkin

1/2 cup heavy whipping cream

2 pinches ground cinnamon

3 pinches ground nutmeg

Coarse salt and black pepper, to taste

1 pound penne rigate or rigatoni pasta, cooked until al dente

Romano or Parmigiano cheese, for grating over pasta

In a deep pot over medium heat, pour in 1 drizzle of oil and brown sausage in it. Remove to paper towel-lined plate to drain and return pan to heat. Add second drizzle of oil to pan and sauté onion and garlic 5 minutes, till soft and sweet. Add bay leaf, sage, and wine to pot. Reduce wine for 2 minutes. Add broth and pumpkin and combine, stirring sauce until it comes to a bubble. Return sausage to pan, reduce heat, and stir in cream. Season with cinnamon, nutmeg, and salt and pepper and simmer 5 minutes.

To serve, return drained, cooked pasta to the pot you cooked it in. Remove bay leaf from sauce and pour sauce over pasta. Toss pasta and sauce 1 or 2 minutes over low heat so pasta can absorb flavors. Top bowls of pasta with freshly grated Parmigiano or Romano cheese.

Pizza Pasta Supreme

SERVES 4 TO 6

1 tablespoon extra-virgin olive oil (once
    around the pan)
1 pound Italian sweet sausage, bulk or cut
    loose from casing
2 ounces pepperoni slices, cut into strips
1 small cooking or boiling onion, chopped fine
1 small sweet Italian pepper (cubanelle), or
    1/2 bell pepper, seeded and chopped
6 mushroom caps, button or crimini, chopped
2 sprigs fresh oregano, chopped, or
    1/2 teaspoon (a couple of pinches), dried
1 can (14 ounces) pizza sauce
1 can (14 ounces) crushed tomatoes
1 pound wagon-wheel pasta, cooked until
    al dente
Grated mozzarella cheese, for topping

Place deep skillet over medium-high heat and add oil; heat 30 seconds. Add sausage and brown, 3 to 5 minutes. Add pepperoni and cook 1 minute more. Add onion, pepper, mushrooms, and oregano and cover; cook 3 to 5 minutes, stirring occasionally. Add pizza sauce and crushed tomatoes. Stir and reduce heat to low. Simmer until ready to toss with pasta.

To assemble, toss sauce and pasta together and transfer to serving dish. Top pasta with cheese and serve with a tossed green salad and crusty bread or garlic toast.

Grandpa's Ziti with Sausage and Cannellini Beans

SERVES 4 TO 6

1 1/2 pounds bulk Italian sausage, 3/4 pound sweet and 3/4 pound hot (available at the butcher counter)

2 tablespoons extra-virgin olive oil (twice around the pan)

4 to 6 cloves garlic, minced

1 small white onion, finely chopped

1 can (28 ounces) crushed tomatoes

1 can (14 ounces) Italian-style diced tomatoes

20 fresh basil leaves, rough cut or torn

1 can (15 ounces) cannellini beans, drained and rinsed

1/2 pound ziti rigate (with lines), cooked until al dente

Grated Parmigiano or Romano, for the table

In a deep skillet or frying pan, brown crumbled sausage over medium-high heat. Remove from pan to a paper towel-lined dish to drain. Return the pan to heat. Reduce heat to medium low. Add olive oil, garlic, and onion and cook 5 minutes, until the onion softens. Add tomatoes, basil, and beans. Heat through. Return sausage to sauce. Drain pasta. Combine with sauce and serve, with plenty of grated cheese, bread, and a green salad.

Pan-Roasted Sausage, Peppers, Onions, and Potatoes

SERVES 4

12 to 15 small fingerling potatoes, quartered, or
    6 red new potatoes, cut in wedges
Generous drizzle extra-virgin olive oil
Montreal Steak Seasoning by McCormick, or
    coarse salt and black pepper
2 tablespoons chopped fresh rosemary (2 sprigs,
    stripped and chopped)
A sprinkle sweet Hungarian paprika (optional)
4 links Italian sweet sausage
4 links Italian hot sausage
1 tablespoon extra-virgin olive oil (once around
    the pan)
2 Italian cubanelle peppers (long and light green
    in color), seeded and sliced
1 small red bell pepper, seeded and sliced
1 medium onion, peeled and sliced
6 cloves garlic, cracked from skins and left whole
A handful chopped fresh flat-leaf parsley
A splash (about 2 tablespoons) juice from
    pickled, hot, sliced cherry peppers
4 slices hot cherry peppers, finely chopped
Warm, crusty bread, for mopping up plates

Preheat a nonstick skillet over medium-high heat. In a bowl, toss potatoes with a drizzle of oil—enough to thinly coat all of the wedges—and sprinkle with Montreal seasoning, rosemary, and paprika. Add potatoes to hot nonstick pan, cover, and cook 15 minutes, turning occasionally.

Cut sausages into large chunks.

Heat a large, deep skillet over medium-high heat. Add the 1 tablespoon oil and brown sausages on all sides. Drain excess oil. Add peppers, onion, and garlic. Cover pan and cook 10 minutes more.

Uncover and toss in the parsley, the splash of cherry pepper juice, and the chopped cherry peppers. Add cooked potatoes, shaking pan to combine all ingredients. Remove pan from heat and serve sausages right from the pot with lots of crusty bread.

Meatloaf Patties and Smashed Potatoes with Scallions

MAKES 4 PATTIES AND 3 TO 4 SERVINGS POTATOES

SMASHED POTATOES

8 to 10 small white- or red-skinned potatoes, quartered
1/2 cup sour cream or reduced-fat sour cream
2 splashes low-fat milk (about 1/4 cup)
2 tablespoons butter
4 scallions, sliced thin
Coarse salt and pepper, to taste

PATTIES

1/2 cup plain bread crumbs
1 teaspoon ground cumin (1/3 palmful)
1/2 teaspoon allspice
1 splash low-fat milk (about 1/8 cup)
1 large egg, beaten
1 small boiling onion, chopped fine
1 tablespoon Worcestershire sauce
1 rounded tablespoon tomato paste
A handful chopped fresh flat-leaf parsley
1 pound 90% lean ground beef sirloin
A drizzle extra-virgin olive oil or nonstick cooking spray

5-MINUTE SMOKY GRAVY

2 tablespoons butter
2 tablespoons all-purpose flour (a handful)
1 can (14 ounces) low-sodium beef broth
2 tablespoons smoky barbecue sauce
1 rounded tablespoon tomato paste
Freshly ground black pepper, to taste

Bring a medium-size deep pot of salted water to a boil. Add potatoes and cook 10 to 12 minutes, till fork tender. When potatoes are tender, drain and return to hot pot. Add sour cream, milk, butter, and scallions and smash to desired consistency with potato masher. Season with salt and pepper, to taste.

While potatoes cook, combine the bread crumbs, ground cumin, and allspice in a large bowl. Add the next 7 ingredients and form 4 large, oval-shaped patties 1 inch thick. Preheat large nonstick skillet over medium-high heat. Rub with a little oil or spray with nonstick cooking spray. Add patties to pan and cook, 5 to 6 minutes, turn, reduce heat, and cook 10 minutes more. Remove patties from pan.

To make gravy add butter to pan and melt. Sprinkle in flour and cook 1 to 2 minutes over medium heat, using a whisk to combine with butter. Slowly add broth, stirring until combined. Bring to a boil. Reduce broth, 2 to 3 minutes. Whisk in barbecue sauce and tomato paste. Remove from heat and season with black pepper to taste. Cover with aluminum foil until ready to serve.

Serve patties and potatoes with generous amounts of gravy and a green salad.

Swedish Meatballs and Egg Noodles
SERVES 2 TO 3

MEATBALLS

1 pound ground chuck, or ground beef, pork,
 and veal mix
1/2 cup bread crumbs (a couple of handfuls)
1 egg, beaten
1 small onion, finely chopped
A few drops Worcestershire sauce
Salt and black pepper, to taste

SAUCE

3 tablespoons butter
2 tablespoons all-purpose flour
1/2 cup dry sherry
1 cup beef broth
Black pepper, to taste
1 teaspoon Dijon mustard
1/2 cup sour cream, or reduced-fat sour cream

1/2 pound wide egg noodles, cooked following
 directions on package
1 tablespoon butter, cut into small pieces
A handful chopped fresh parsley

Place a pot of lightly salted water on the stove to boil for your egg noodles and cook them once the water has come to a rapid boil. While waiting for water to boil, make meatballs and sauce.

To bake meatballs, preheat oven to 400 degrees F. Mix ingredients for meatballs in a medium-size bowl. Form bite-size balls and place on nonstick cookie sheet. Place meatballs in oven and bake 12 minutes.

To cook meatballs on the stovetop, preheat nonstick frying pan over medium heat. Mix ingredients for meatballs in a medium-size bowl. Form bite-size balls and add directly to the pan as you roll them. Once the last ball has been rolled, give the pan a good shake and place a lid or aluminum foil over the top. Cook meatballs 10 to 12 minutes, turning them occasionally by giving the pan a good shake. Remove meatballs to a paper towel-lined plate, wipe out pan, and return to heat to make the sauce.

To make sauce, melt butter over medium heat. Sprinkle in flour and continuously whisk until a smooth paste is formed and mixture begins to darken a bit. Slowly add sherry while continuing to whisk sauce; cook until sherry reduces by half. Add broth in a slow stream and continue to stir until sauce thickens enough to lightly coat the back of a spoon and is glossy in appearance. Turn off heat and whisk in pepper, Dijon mustard, and sour cream until incorporated evenly.

Toss hot egg noodles with butter and parsley. Coat meatballs in sauce and serve over noodles.

Jessica's Groovy Goulash
SERVES 4

1/2 pound elbow macaroni, cooked until
    al dente
1 tablespoon extra-virgin olive oil (once around
    the pan)
2 pounds ground beef chuck, or ground beef,
    pork, and veal mix
1 medium onion, chopped
3 cloves garlic, minced
1 tablespoon ground cumin (half a palmful)
1 tablespoon sweet paprika (half a palmful)
Salt and pepper, to taste
2 tablespoons chopped fresh marjoram
    (a palmful), or 1 teaspoon dried
1 can (14 ounces) crushed tomatoes or chunky
    crushed tomatoes
1/2 cup sour cream, or reduced-fat sour cream
Chopped fresh parsley, for garnish

While the water is heating for the pasta, heat a deep skillet over medium-high heat. Brown ground meat in a little olive oil, breaking meat up with a spoon. Add onion, garlic, and seasonings to the pot and cook another 5 minutes. Mix in tomatoes and heat through, then stir in sour cream.

Drain cooked macaroni and add to pot, combining meat and macaroni. Garnish with parsley.

Serve with a spinach salad or a fruit and cheese board of Leyden or smoked gouda, bosc pears, and red grapes.

Chili Mac
SERVES 4

1 1/2 pounds lean ground sirloin

1 tablespoon extra-virgin olive oil (once around the pan)

1 medium yellow-skinned onion, finely chopped

4 cloves garlic

1 can (14 ounces) crushed tomatoes

2 to 3 tablespoons chili powder (a palmful)

1 to 1 1/2 tablespoons ground cumin (half a palmful)

6 drops Red Hot or Tabasco sauce (cayenne pepper sauce)

Coarse salt and black pepper, to taste

1/2 pound (half a box) elbow pasta or other shape, cooked until al dente

1 cup shredded Monterey Jack, cheddar or smoked cheddar cheese (optional)

Chopped tomato and scallions, to garnish (optional)

In a deep frying pan or saucepot, brown ground sirloin in olive oil over medium-high heat. Add onion and garlic. Cook until the onion is translucent, about 5 minutes.

Add crushed tomatoes and seasonings. Bring to a boil, then lower heat and simmer until ready to serve.

To serve, combine cooked, drained pasta with chili. Top chili mac with cheese, if you like. For a kosher meal, just hold the cheese and sprinkle with chopped tomato and scallions.

Stove-Top Stuffed Peppers

SERVES 4

QUICK TOMATO SAUCE

6 cloves garlic, minced

1/2 teaspoon crushed red pepper flakes
(a few pinches)

2 tablespoons extra-virgin olive oil (twice
around the pan)

1 tablespoon chopped fresh oregano, or
1 teaspoon dried

1 can (15 ounces) low-salt beef broth

3 ounces tomato paste (half a small can)

1 can (28 ounces) crushed tomatoes

10 to 12 fresh basil leaves, chopped

A handful chopped fresh flat-leaf parsley

STUFFED PEPPERS

1 cup short-grain rice

6 medium bell peppers, red or green or
3 of each

1 1/2 pounds ground chuck, or ground beef,
pork, and veal mix

2 tablespoons extra-virgin olive oil

1 bell pepper, chopped

1 medium onion, chopped

1 cup Quick Tomato Sauce

1/2 cup frozen peas

6 ounces fresh mozzarella, diced

Salt and pepper, to taste

Put 2 pots of salted water on the stove to boil before you begin this recipe—1 small pot with 2 cups water and 1 large pot with 4 cups water.

In a saucepot over medium heat, sauté garlic and crushed red pepper in olive oil for 1 or 2 minutes to begin sauce. Add remaining ingredients, bring to a bubble, reduce heat, and let simmer over low heat.

Add rice to small pot of boiling, salted water. Cover, reduce heat, and simmer 20 minutes.

Cut tops off peppers and scoop out seeds. Cut an X in the bottom of each pepper. Place peppers in large pot of boiling, salted water, cover, reduce heat, and simmer 10 minutes. Remove peppers and drain upside down on paper towels.

In a skillet over medium-high heat, brown ground meat in olive oil. Add bell pepper and onion, cover, and cook 5 minutes, stirring occasionally. Reduce heat to low. When rice is done, add to meat and stir in 1 cup of sauce, peas, mozzarella, and salt and pepper to taste. Remove filling from heat. Place the pot you emptied after cooking the peppers back on the stove over low heat. Cover the bottom of the pot with a layer of sauce. Stuff peppers with filling and place upright in sauce in pot. Top each pepper with a little extra sauce and cover to keep warm until ready to serve.

Saucy Pepper Steak

SERVES 4

1 cup white rice, 4 to 6 servings, cooked
   following directions on bag or box

1 pound sirloin 1 inch thick
2 tablespoons soy sauce (a glug)
2 tablespoons vegetable or peanut oil
3 bell peppers, a mixture of red, yellow, and
   green, split and seeded
1 medium white onion, peeled
1 tablespoon vegetable or peanut oil
2 cloves garlic, crushed
1 inch fresh gingerroot, grated, or 1/2 teaspoon
   ground ginger

SAUCE
A splash of rice wine, dry cooking sherry, or rice
   wine vinegar (about 2 tablespoons)
1 cup low-sodium beef broth
1 teaspoon (1/3 palmful) Chinese five spice
   blend (found on spice aisle)
1 rounded tablespoon tomato paste
1 rounded teaspoon cornstarch dissolved in 2 or
   3 tablespoons warm water
Black pepper, to taste

Start cooking rice.

Cut meat into bite-size cubes or strips. Coat meat in soy sauce and oil. Cube seeded peppers into bite-size chunks. Dice the onion.

Place a deep, nonstick skillet over high heat. When the pan is hot, add meat and cook 5 to 6 minutes, until meat is cooked through but still tender. Remove meat to serving dish and return pan to heat.

Add the 1 tablespoon oil to the pan and when the oil smokes, stir in peppers. Stir-fry peppers for 2 or 3 minutes. Add onion and garlic and ginger and cook 2 or 3 minutes more. Remove vegetables to serving dish.

Return pan to stove. To make sauce, add rice wine, sherry, or rice wine vinegar and scrape up pan drippings. Add broth and spice blend, then tomato paste and cornstarch. Bring sauce to a bubble and stir with whisk until it begins to thicken.

Remove from heat. Season with black pepper. Add meat and vegetables back to pan and toss to coat. Transfer cooked rice to serving dish and top with completed pepper steak.

Beef Ragout and Oven-Roasted Potatoes

POTATOES

16 small fingerling potatoes, or 8 small white potatoes, peeled

Extra-virgin olive oil, to coat (a couple of tablespoons)

Montreal Steak Seasoning by McCormick, or coarse salt and black pepper, to taste

A sprinkle paprika

SAUCE

3 tablespoons butter

2 tablespoons all-purpose flour

1/2 cup dry sherry

1 cup low-sodium beef broth

Black pepper, to taste

1/2 teaspoon allspice (a couple of pinches)

A palmful chopped fresh flat-leaf parsley

RAGOUT

1 pound top sirloin, 1 inch thick, cut into 2-inch cubes

1/2 tablespoon butter

A drizzle extra-virgin olive oil

Montreal Steak Seasoning, or coarse salt and black pepper, to taste

VEGETABLES

1 tablespoon extra-virgin olive oil

8 button mushrooms, cleaned and trimmed

1 medium onion, coarsely chopped

1 medium green bell pepper, diced

A splash of sherry or beef broth

Preheat oven to 450 degrees F. Coat potatoes in olive oil and seasonings. Scatter potatoes in shallow baking dish and place on middle rack of oven to roast for 25 minutes, or until tender.

To make sauce, melt butter over medium heat. Sprinkle in flour and continuously whisk until a smooth paste is formed and mixture begins to darken a bit. Slowly add sherry while continuing to whisk sauce, and cook until sherry reduces by half. Add broth in a slow stream and continue to stir until sauce thickens enough to lightly coat the back of a spoon and is glossy in appearance. Turn off heat and whisk in pepper, allspice, and parsley.

Pat meat dry with paper towels. Heat butter and a touch of oil in a skillet over high heat. When pan begins to smoke, add meat and cook

3 minutes on each side, giving the pan a shake frequently and reducing heat a touch if pan continues to smoke excessively. Remove meat from pan, transferring to a serving dish, and sprinkle with seasoning.

Return pan to stove and reduce heat to medium-high. Add olive oil and vegetables and sauté, frequently shaking pan vigorously to keep vegetables from sticking. Cook 3 to 5 minutes, until just tender. Add a splash of sherry or broth to the pan and reduce, using it to loosen any drippings. Add meat back to pan and distribute sauce evenly over meat and vegetables.

Remove potatoes from oven and cut each in half. To serve, scoop meat and vegetables into shallow bowls and garnish bowls with a few roasted potatoes set into the meat and sauce.

Smothered Beef Steaks
with Mushrooms and Onions

SERVES 2

1 pound sirloin steak, 1 inch thick, cut into
   2 pieces

1/4 cup Worcestershire sauce

A drizzle extra-virgin olive oil

Montreal Steak Seasoning by McCormick, or
   coarse salt and black pepper, to taste

2 tablespoons butter

1 large sweet onion, such as Vidalia or Texas
   Sweet, sliced very thin

12 crimini mushroom caps, sliced thin

1/2 cup dry sherry

1/2 cup beef broth

Salt and pepper, to taste

2 slices white bread, toasted and cut corner
   to corner

Pat steaks dry. Brush with Worcestershire on each side. Rub with oil and Montreal seasoning.

Heat a skillet over medium to medium-high heat. Add butter and onion to pan. Cook onion 5 minutes, till soft. Add mushrooms and cook another 10 minutes, till onions caramelize and mushrooms are tender.

Heat a grill pan or large nonstick griddle over high heat. Cook steaks 5 minutes on each side for medium. Remove from heat and let stand 5 minutes more.

To finish onions and mushrooms, add sherry to pan and scrape up pan drippings. Add broth and season with salt and pepper to taste.

To serve, place steaks on toast points and cover with onions and mushrooms.

Weeknight Spaghetti and Meatballs

SERVES 4

1 pound ground beef, 93% lean

1 egg, beaten

1/2 small cooking or boiling onion, finely
    chopped

2 cloves garlic, minced

1/4 cup grated Parmigiano (a handful)

1/2 cup Italian bread crumbs (2 handfuls)

Ground black pepper, to taste

1 tablespoon extra-virgin olive oil (once around
    the pan)

1/2 cup beef broth or dry red wine (a couple of
    splashes)

1 can (28 ounces) crushed tomatoes

1/2 teaspoon (2 shakes) crushed red pepper
    flakes

2 sprigs fresh oregano, chopped, or
    2 pinches dried

A palmful chopped fresh flat-leaf parsley

3/4 pound spaghetti, cooked until al dente,
    about 8 minutes

Grated Parmigiano cheese and garlic bread, for
    the table

Combine meat, egg, onion, garlic, grated cheese, bread crumbs, and a little pepper in a bowl.

Heat a deep nonstick skillet over medium-high heat and drizzle in oil. Roll small balls and drop into hot pan. When all the meat is rolled and in the pan, give the pan a good shake and cover. Cook meatballs for 8 minutes, giving the pan a good shake frequently to keep meat from burning. If balls are browning too quickly, reduce heat a little.

Add broth or wine and let reduce for 1 or 2 minutes. Add tomatoes and red pepper flakes, then oregano and parsley. Simmer until pasta is ready. Toss pasta with sauce and serve with garlic bread and grated cheese for topping.

Beef Stroganoff

SERVES 4

2 tablespoons all-purpose flour (a handful)

1 tablespoon mild Hungarian paprika (half a palmful)

Coarse salt and black pepper, to taste

1 pound beef sirloin, 1/2-inch thick, cut into bite-size cubes or strips

2 tablespoons extra-virgin olive oil (two turns around the pan)

1/2 cup dry sherry (a couple of glugs)

1 cup beef broth (about half a 14-ounce can)

1/2 cup sour cream, or reduced-fat sour cream

1/2 pound egg noodles, or 1 package spaetzel dumplings, cooked following directions on package

1 pat butter (about 1/2 tablespoon) to toss with noodles or spaetzel

1/2 cup baby sweet gherkin pickles or cornichons, finely chopped (optional)

Chopped fresh chives or fresh parsley, to garnish (optional)

Mix flour, paprika, and salt and pepper on a plate and turn meat in mixture to coat evenly.

Heat a skillet over medium-high heat and add oil. When oil is hot, brown meat for 5 to 6 minutes. Add sherry and scrape up pan drippings. Reduce sherry for 2 or 3 minutes, then add broth. Simmer 5 minutes, then thicken sauce with sour cream and remove from heat.

Serve meat over egg noodles or spaetzel tossed with a touch of butter. Garnish with finely chopped pickles and chives or parsley, if you like it authentic.

Beef Burgundy

SERVES 2 TO 3

1/4 pound pancetta (Italian rolled, cured pork), or center-cut bacon, chopped

1 tablespoon extra-virgin olive oil (1 turn around the pan)

1 pound sirloin steak, cut into 1-inch cubes

3 tablespoons all-purpose flour

Montreal Steak Seasoning by McCormick, or salt and pepper, to taste

1 bay leaf, fresh or dried

6 crimini mushroom caps, chopped

4 fresh shiitake mushroom caps, sliced thin

1 carrot, peeled and chopped

2 shallots, chopped

3 cloves garlic, chopped fine

4 sprigs fresh thyme, leaves stripped and chopped fine

1 cup dry red wine

1 cup beef broth

12 ounces egg noodles, cooked and tossed with a little melted butter and parsley

In a heavy, deep skillet, brown pancetta in 1 tablespoon oil over medium-high heat. Dredge steak in flour seasoned with Montreal seasoning or salt and pepper. Add meat and bay leaf to pan and brown meat on all sides. Remove meat to a warm platter.

Add mushrooms, carrot, shallots, garlic, and thyme to pan. Sauté over medium heat 5 minutes, stirring frequently. Add wine and broth to pan and scrape up drippings. Bring to a boil and reduce liquids, 5 to 7 minutes. Return meat to pan and cook 2 to 3 minutes more. Adjust seasonings and remove bay leaf. Serve beef over buttered and parsleyed egg noodles.

Elsie's Braciole

SERVES 2

4 slices beef braciole (beef thinly sliced from
top round)

Coarse salt and black pepper, or Montreal Steak
Seasoning by McCormick

4 slices prosciutto (from the deli counter)

3/4 cup plain bread crumbs (a couple handfuls)

1/4 cup milk (2 splashes)

1/3 cup grated Parmigiano or Romano cheese

1 small cooking or boiling onion, minced

1/4 cup chopped, fresh flat-leaf parsley
(a handful)

1/2 cup chopped arugula (1/2 bunch—add extra
to salad greens)

1/8 teaspoon (3 pinches) ground nutmeg

Plain round toothpicks

2 tablespoons extra-virgin olive oil

2 cloves garlic, cracked and removed from skin
with a whack from the flat of a knife

1 cup dry white wine (3 or 4 glugs)

6 to 8 crimini mushrooms, finely chopped

2 tablespoons butter

2 tablespoons all-purpose flour (a handful)

1 cup beef broth

1 tablespoon tomato paste

Coarse black pepper, to taste

1/2 pound gnocchi, cooked and drained

Season meat with a little salt and pepper or
Montreal seasoning. Top each piece of meat
with a slice of prosciutto.

In a small bowl, moisten bread crumbs with
milk and allow liquid to be absorbed. Add
cheese, onion, parsley, arugula, and nutmeg to
bread crumbs and combine. Spread a thin layer
of stuffing down the center of each piece of
meat. Roll meat and secure with toothpicks.

Heat oil in a heavy nonstick skillet over medium-
high heat. Add garlic and meat rolls. Brown meat
on all sides for 5 or 6 minutes, then add wine.
Reduce heat to low, partially cover pan and
reduce wine by half over the next few minutes.

While meat simmers, sauté mushrooms in butter over medium-high 2 or 3 minutes. Sprinkle
pan with flour and cook 1 minute more, whisking constantly. Whisk in broth, tomato paste,
and pepper to taste. Allow sauce to thicken a
bit, then pour over meat cooking in wine.
Continue to simmer meat until ready to serve.

To assemble, place gnocchi on dinner plates
with meat alongside. Remove picks and spoon
sauce over gnocchi and meat. A salad and warm
dinner rolls complete your meal.

Veal Scallopini al Limone

SERVES UP TO 4

8 veal loin cutlets (1 1/4 pounds)

large plastic food storage bag

1/2 cup all-purpose flour (a couple handfuls),
     plus 1 tablespoon (a sprinkle)

Salt and pepper, to taste

2 tablespoons extra-virgin olive oil (2 turns
     around the pan)

3 tablespoons butter, total

1 large shallot, chopped fine

1/4 to 1/3 cup dry white wine (2 splashes)

Juice of 1 lemon

1/2 cup beef broth

A few grinds black pepper, to taste

4 thin slices lemon, to garnish

A handful fresh flat-leaf parsley, chopped fine

1 package (9 to 10 ounces) rice pilaf or white
     and wild rice blend, prepared following
     directions on box

Place cutlets, 2 at a time, in a large food storage bag and pound thin with mallet. Pile cutlets up on a work surface. Pour 1/2 cup flour on a plate and season with salt and pepper. Turn cutlets in flour just before adding them to the pan to cook.

Heat 1 tablespoon extra-virgin olive oil in a large skillet over medium-high heat. Add 1 tablespoon of butter to pan and sauté 4 scallopini cutlets, 2 minutes on each side; remove to warm platter. Repeat with remaining cutlets.

Once veal is browned, add remaining 2 tablespoons butter and shallot to pan. Reduce heat to medium low and sauté 2 minutes. Add a tablespoon flour to pan and cook 1 minute more. Add wine and lemon juice to pan and scrape up drippings with a whisk. Reduce wine and juice by half, about 2 minutes. Season with pepper to taste. Add broth and, whisking occasionally, thicken sauce 2 minutes more.

Pour sauce on warm dinner plates, top with scallopini, and garnish with lemon slices and chopped fresh parsley. Serve with prepared rice pilaf or white and wild rice blend and a green salad.

Stuffed Veal Chops

SERVES 4

4 veal chops, 1 inch thick

4 ounces fontina cheese, sliced thin

4 slices prosciutto di Parma

4 crimini mushroom caps, sliced thin

1 teaspoon butter

1 sprig fresh thyme, chopped

Salt and pepper, to taste

2 tablespoons extra-virgin olive oil (2 turns
     around the pan)

3 tablespoons butter

1 shallot, chopped fine

2 sprigs fresh rosemary, chopped fine

1 1/2 tablespoons all-purpose flour (a palmful)

1 cup dry vermouth

1 cup beef broth

4 pieces garlic bread or toasted, buttered white
     bread, cut corner to corner

Place baking dish in oven and preheat oven to 350 degrees F. Cut a slit in the side of each chop and stuff each with 1 slice fontina and 1 slice prosciutto. Cook sliced mushroom caps 3 minutes in one teaspoon of butter, season with thyme and salt and pepper. Stuff mushrooms into pockets with fontina and ham. Close chops with toothpicks.

Brown chops on each side over medium-high heat in 2 tablespoons olive oil. Season chops with salt and pepper to taste and remove from pan to baking dish in oven to finish cooking, about 10 minutes.

Replace skillet over medium heat and sauté shallot and rosemary in remaining 3 pats butter. Sauté 2 minutes, add flour, and cook 1 minute more. Add vermouth to pan while whisking up pan drippings. Reduce vermouth, 1 minute, and add broth. Simmer sauce 3 minutes and remove from heat. Place chops on garlic bread or buttered toast points and pour sauce over top.

Grandpa Emmanuel's
Veal Cutlets from Gela

SERVES 4

8 veal loin cutlets

1/2 cup all-purpose flour seasoned with salt
and pepper, to taste

2 tablespoons extra-virgin olive oil (1 turn
around the pan)

3 cloves garlic, cracked from skin and crushed
but not chopped

3/4 cup dry white wine (3 glugs)

1 can (14 ounces) diced tomatoes, drained

1 can (14 ounces) quartered artichoke hearts in
water, drained

12 oil-cured black olives, pitted and chopped

Salt and pepper, to taste

12 ounces angel-hair pasta, cooked until al dente

Dredge cutlets in seasoned flour and brown in a large skillet (3 minutes per side) over medium-high heat in oil with cracked garlic cloves—make sure oil is hot before adding cutlets. Add wine and reduce by half, 1 or 2 minutes. Add tomatoes, artichoke hearts, olives, and a little salt and pepper. Cover pan and simmer 3 minutes, then remove from heat.

Place cutlets on warm dinner plates and top with a little cooked tomato and artichoke hearts. Toss pasta with pan drippings and remaining sauce and serve alongside.

Lamb Chops with Rosemary and Warm Cherry Tomato Salad

SERVES 2 TO 3

CHOPS

6 small lamb loin chops

1 tablespoon balsamic vinegar (a splash)

1 tablespoon extra-virgin olive oil (a glug)

2 sprigs fresh rosemary, leaves stripped from stem and chopped fine

1 clove garlic, chopped fine

Montreal Steak Seasoning by McCormick, or salt and pepper, to taste

SALAD

1 large shallot, chopped fine

2 tablespoons extra-virgin oil (2 turns around the pan)

1 pint grape or cherry tomatoes, halved

1/2 cup (2 handfuls) fresh flat-leaf parsley tops, chopped

Coarse salt and black pepper, to taste

Preheat broiler to high or prepare grill.

Combine chops with vinegar, oil, rosemary, and garlic. Season lightly on each side with Montreal seasoning or salt and pepper.

Broil or grill chops 6 inches from heat source, 5 minutes on one side, 3 on the other for rare—up to 6 minutes on the reverse side for medium-well.

In a skillet over medium heat, sauté shallot in oil 3 minutes. Add tomatoes and warm 1 or 2 minutes. Remove from heat and toss with parsley and salt and pepper. Serve salad alongside chops with good bread for mopping up juices.

Rick's Shish Sticks

SERVES 4

1/2 boneless leg of lamb, trimmed of all fat and
connective tissue (2 to 2 1/2 pounds)

3 tablespoons extra-virgin olive oil (2 glugs)

1 large clove garlic, crushed

1 tablespoon ground cumin (a palmful)

1 rounded teaspoon ground coriander
(1/3 palmful)

1 rounded teaspoon sweet paprika (1/2 palmful)

2 sprigs fresh rosemary, chopped fine, or 3
pinches dried rosemary, crushed in the palm
of your hand

Juice of 1 lemon

8 fresh bay leaves (from produce department)

Coarse salt and black pepper, to taste, or
Montreal Steak Seasoning by McCormick
(1/2 palmful)

1 large green bell pepper, seeded and cut
into chunks

6 metal kabob skewers

1 large sweet onion, such as Vidalia or Texas
Sweet, cut into chunks

nonstick cooking spray

Prepared tahini sauce (from the appetizer
section of your market)

8 pita breads, any variety, warmed

Cube lamb into bite-size chunks. Using a small
pan, heat garlic in oil until garlic speaks or pour
olive oil over crushed garlic and heat in
microwave on high for 1 minute. Let cool, then
pour over lamb. Combine cumin, coriander,
paprika, rosemary, lemon juice, bay leaves, and
salt and pepper or Montreal seasoning in a plastic food storage bag. Add lamb, combine well
and let stand 15 minutes.

Thread peppers on one metal skewer, onions on
a second, and spray grill with nonstick cooking
spray. Broil or grill 10 minutes, turning occasionally.

Thread lamb on skewers with 2 bay leaves per
skewer, dividing meat evenly among 4 skewers.
Grill or broil lamb 6 inches from heat source on
hot grill or under broiler preheated to high.
Cook lamb 4 to 5 minutes on each side for
medium-rare.

Spread warmed pita breads with tahini sauce
and add lamb and veggies. Serve with a chunky
vegetable salad or storebought tabbouleh salad.

Seafood

My mama's recipes for seafood and pasta
inspire me. Infused with garlic and bathed in
olive oil and white wine, these Italian comfort
foods are light and oh so good.

For a zesty treat, try Quick Creole Shrimp,
a recipe from my dad's family in Louisiana
where they know about shrimp. I warn you,
this is so good you might have to make
enough for seconds!

Fish Fry

SERVES 4

1 1/2 pounds haddock fillets
1 cup all-purpose flour
1 tablespoon Old Bay seasoning
Salt and pepper, to taste
4 large eggs, beaten
canola oil for frying, about 2 cups
1 large ripe lemon, cut into wedges

Cut haddock into 6- or 7-ounce pieces. Turn fish in flour seasoned with Old Bay and a little salt and pepper. Shake off excess flour and set aside.

Place a shallow dish with beaten eggs near the stovetop. Heat a 1/2-inch layer of vegetable oil in a large nonstick skillet over medium to medium-high heat. Dip fish in egg and fry in small batches, 3 minutes per side, until golden. Remove fish to platter. Wipe pan clean and heat fresh oil for each batch of fillets.

Serve with wedges of lemon and an Oil and Vinegar Slaw Salad (recipe follows).

Oil and Vinegar Slaw Salad
SERVES 4

1 pound (a 16-ounce bag) shredded cabbage slaw
    mix (available in produce section)
3 radishes, washed and shredded
A handful fresh flat-leaf parsley, chopped fine
3 tablespoons vegetable or canola oil (a couple
    of glugs)
1 1/2 tablespoons white vinegar or apple cider
    vinegar (3 splashes)
2 tablespoons honey (2 drizzles)
1 teaspoon celery seed (1/3 palmful)
Coarse salt and black pepper, to taste

Combine all ingredients, adjust seasoning to taste, and let stand 15 minutes before serving.

Crab Cakes and Roasted Red Pepper Sauce

MAKES 10 2-INCH CAKES

1 1/2 cups cracker meal (found near bread crumbs in supermarket)

1/2 cup milk (2 splashes)

3 cans (6 ounces each) lump white crab, drained very well

A few pinches coarse salt

1 rounded teaspoon Old Bay seasoning

1 tablespoon baking powder

A handful chopped fresh flat-leaf parsley

1 stalk celery from heart of stalk, chopped very fine

Zest of 1 lemon

1 tablespoon Worcestershire sauce (take the jigger top off and add a splash)

6 drops hot sauce, Tabasco or Red Hot

2 tablespoons mayonnaise, or ranch dressing

1 large egg, beaten

Vegetable oil, for frying

1 lemon, cut into wedges

Place cracker meal in a bowl and moisten with milk. Add crabmeat, salt, Old Bay seasoning, baking powder, parsley, celery, lemon zest, Worcestershire, Tabasco, mayonnaise or dressing, and beaten egg. Combine crab cake mixture and form into 8 patties. Fry in hot oil (1/2-inch deep) over medium-high heat until golden, 3 to 5 minutes on each side.

Serve with lemon wedges and Red Pepper Sauce (recipe follows).

Roasted Red Pepper Sauce

One 14-ounce jar roasted red peppers, drained,
    or 3 homemade roasted peppers
6 to 10 drops Tabasco, depending on your
    palate (6 for mild, 10 for hot)
Juice of 1/2 lemon
1/2 teaspoon celery salt, or to taste

Combine all ingredients in a food processor and pulse until a smooth, loose paste is formed.

Tuna Cakes and Spicy Mayo

MAKES 10 2-INCH CAKES

3 cloves roasted garlic (remaining from Spicy Mayo recipe)

1 cup prepared instant mashed potatoes, plain or roasted garlic flavor

2 cans (6 ounces each) Albacore tuna, drained and flaked

1/4 cup grated Parmigiano cheese (2 handfuls)

1/2 cup Italian bread crumbs (4 handfuls), divided in half

1 large egg, beaten

A handful fresh flat-leaf parsley, chopped

Montreal Steak Seasoning by McCormick, or coarse salt and black pepper, to taste

1/4 cup all-purpose flour (2 handfuls)

Light olive or canola oil for frying

First, prepare the Spicy Mayo (recipe on following page).

Combine first 8 ingredients, using only half the bread crumbs. Form into 8 patties. Turn patties in flour, then in remaining bread crumbs. Fry patties 3 to 5 minutes on each side in hot oil (1/2-inch deep) over medium-high heat until golden. Drain on paper towels. Serve cakes with a spoonful of Spicy Mayo on top.

Spicy Mayo

6 cloves garlic, whole in skin
A drizzle extra-virgin olive oil or nonstick
    cooking spray
1 tablespoon capers (a palmful)
6 drops Tabasco Sauce
Juice of 1/2 lemon
A palmful fresh flat-leaf parsley
1/2 cup mayonnaise
A few grinds coarse black pepper

Leave garlic cloves in skin, cut off ends, and coat with a touch of olive oil or cooking spray. Wrap in aluminum foil and place in small skillet over medium-high heat. Cover tightly and pan roast 12 minutes, turning once, until soft. Remove garlic and let cool. Push cloves free of skin and place 3 cloves in food processor. Add capers, Tabasco, lemon juice, parsley, mayonnaise and pepper. Pulse until ingredients are well combined. Remove from processor and set aside.

Salmon Cakes
MAKES 10 2-INCH CAKES

SALMON CAKES

2 cans (6 ounces each) salmon, drained well
    and flaked with a fork
1 cup cracker meal
2 eggs, beaten
1 rounded teaspoon Old Bay seasoning
1/2 red bell pepper, seeded and chopped fine
15 to 20 blades fresh chives, chopped fine
Grated zest of 1 lemon
Coarse salt and black pepper, to taste
Canola oil, for frying
6 ounces mixed baby greens
1 lemon, cut into wedges

LEMON DILL MAYONNAISE

1/2 cup mayonnaise or reduced-fat mayonnaise
Juice of 1 lemon
2 tablespoons capers (a handful), chopped
A handful fresh dill, chopped (about 2
    tablespoons)

Combine first 8 ingredients and form 10 2-inch patties. Heat canola oil (1/2-inch) in a deep skillet over medium-high heat. Fry cakes in hot oil, 5 at a time, for 3 to 5 minutes on each side or until deep golden. Drain on paper towels.

Combine ingredients for mayonnaise in a small bowl. Serve cakes on a bed of mixed baby greens with lemon wedges and a few spoonfuls of mayonnaise to garnish.

Poached Salmon with Herb Sauce

SERVES 4

This recipe can easily be adjusted to make from 1 to 10 servings in less than 15 minutes. For 1 or 2 pieces of salmon, just cut back on the poaching liquid and use half the sauce recipe.

Four 6-ounce pieces frozen salmon fillet
 (available in individual portion packets at
 fish counter of market)
1 1/2 cups dry white wine or chicken broth
1 1/2 cups water
1 bay leaf
A few sprigs each, fresh dill, tarragon, and chives,
 tied into a bundle with a bit of kitchen
 string (your own preference of fresh herbs
 may be substituted)

HERB SAUCE (Makes 1 cup)
1 cup sour cream, or reduced-fat sour cream
2 tablespoons tarragon or white wine vinegar,
 or distilled white vinegar
A few sprigs each, about 2 to 3 tablespoons
 total, chopped dill, chives, and tarragon
1 tablespoon capers, chopped (optional)
Salt and/or black pepper, to taste
1/2 seedless European cucumber, thinly sliced
Sliced pumpernickel bread or split rolls

Defrost salmon fillets on low setting in microwave for 5 minutes, or by removing salmon from freezer and placing in refrigerator 1 day ahead of preparation.

Place salmon fillets in a large, deep skillet and add wine or broth and water to pan. Add bay leaf and the bundle of fresh herbs. Place pan over high heat and bring water to a boil. Reduce heat to medium low and cover pan. Poach salmon for 8 to 10 minutes, or until fish is firm and opaque. Remove from pan and let cool.

Combine sauce ingredients in a bowl. Serve salmon warm or cold with herb sauce, sliced cucumbers, and pumpernickel bread or split rolls. To assemble, place sauce on bread, top with cucumbers and salmon, and eat as you would an open-face sandwich.

Red Snapper Livornese
and Warm Green Bean Salad

SERVES 4

For the Giardanos.

Four 6- to 8-ounce pieces red snapper filet,
    rinsed and dried
A few pinches coarse salt
$1/2$ cup all-purpose flour
$1/2$ teaspoon Old Bay seasoning ($1/4$ palmful)
2 tablespoons extra-virgin olive oil (2 turns
    around the pan)

LIVORNESE SAUCE

1 tablespoon extra-virgin olive oil (1 turn around
    the pan)
4 large cloves garlic, chopped
$1/2$ cup chopped fresh flat-leaf parsley
    (2 handfuls)
1 bay leaf, fresh or dried
1 cup dry white wine (3 glugs)
1 can (28 ounces) diced tomatoes, drained

Lightly salt snapper fillets. Coat fillets in flour seasoned with Old Bay. Heat 2 tablespoons oil over medium to medium-high heat. Brown snapper 2 or 3 minutes (skin side down first) on each side and remove from heat.

Return pan to stove over medium heat. Add 1 tablespoon oil and garlic. Cook garlic 1 minute, stirring constantly. Add parsley, bay leaf, and wine to pan. Reduce liquid a minute more. Return fish to pan and add tomatoes. Cover, reduce heat to a simmer, and cook 10 minutes.

Serve with crusty bread, steamed new potatoes, and Warm Green Bean Salad (recipe follows).

Warm Green Bean Salad
SERVES 4

1 pound fresh green beans, trimmed
1 cup water
2 ounces pine nuts (pignoli), toasted
1 small shallot, chopped fine
3 tablespoons extra-virgin olive oil
1 tablespoon red wine vinegar (a splash)
1/2 teaspoon sugar (a couple of pinches)
Coarse salt and black pepper, to taste

Steam green beans, 5 minutes in a covered skillet over medium heat in 1 cup of water. Drain beans and transfer to a shallow dish.

Sprinkle green beans with toasted pine nuts. Place shallot in a small dish and cover with oil. Heat in microwave 1 minute on high. Let oil stand 2 or 3 minutes, then whisk in vinegar and sugar. Drizzle warm dressing over green beans and season with salt and pepper to taste.

Fish Provençal

SERVES 4

3 tablespoons extra-virgin olive oil
(3 turns around the pan)
3 cloves garlic, minced
1/2 small onion, chopped fine
1/2 carrot, chopped fine
2 tablespoons total chopped fresh parsley,
sage, rosemary, and thyme, or 1 teaspoon
dried herbes des Provence
1 cup dry white wine
1/2 cup tomato sauce
1 1/2 pounds haddock or cod fillets, rinsed, dried,
and seasoned with a little salt and pepper

In a medium skillet over medium heat, heat 2 tablespoons olive oil. Add garlic, onion, and carrot. Sauté vegetables 3 to 5 minutes. Add herbs and wine to pan and reduce liquid for 1 or 2 minutes. Add tomato sauce and remove from heat.

Preheat broiler to high and place a rack in the center of oven.

In a second large skillet, heat 1 tablespoon oil over medium to medium-high heat. Add fillets to pan, flat side up. Cook 3 minutes, flip, then add sauce to fish. Place skillet under hot broiler and continue cooking until fish is flaky and opaque, 3 to 5 minutes.

My Mama's Baked Fish
SERVES 4

1 1/2 pounds haddock or cod fillets

Cooking spray, or a drizzle of extra-virgin olive oil

A few pinches coarse salt

Juice of 1/2 lemon

1 tablespoon mayonnaise

1 teaspoon Old Bay Seasoning (1/3 palmful)

A few grinds fresh black pepper

1/2 cup plain bread crumbs

1 1/2 tablespoons butter, melted

A palmful chopped fresh flat-leaf parsley

Preheat oven to 425 degrees F.

Spray a baking dish with cooking spray or wipe with a little olive oil. Rinse and dry fish and sprinkle with a little coarse salt. Combine lemon juice, mayonnaise, Old Bay seasoning, and black pepper. Spread a very thin layer of mayonnaise over fish fillets. Sprinkle with bread crumbs and drizzle with butter. Bake 20 minutes, until fish is opaque and flaky. Sprinkle with parsley and serve with Red Potatoes with Olives and Capers (recipe follows).

Red Potatoes with Olives and Capers
SERVES 4

12 small red potatoes, quartered

2 tablespoons chopped capers (a handful)

A handful fresh flat-leaf parsley, chopped

A handful oil-cured black olives, pitted and
chopped

2 tablespoons extra-virgin olive oil

12 blades fresh chives, chopped

Coarse salt and black pepper, to taste

Place potatoes in a pot and cover with water. Bring to a boil and cook 12 minutes, till tender. Drain potatoes and return to pot. Toss with capers, parsley, olives, oil, chives, and salt and pepper to taste.

Anna Maria's Greek Shrimp and Feta Penne

SERVES 4 TO 6

2 pounds large shrimp, peeled and deveined

3 tablespoons extra-virgin olive oil (3 turns around the pan)

6 cloves garlic, minced

1 cup dry white wine

1 can (28 ounces) crushed tomatoes

8 ounces feta cheese, crumbled

Black pepper, to taste

2 tablespoons fresh chopped oregano (2 or 3 sprigs)

A handful chopped fresh flat-leaf parsley

1 pound penne pasta, cooked until al dente, about 8 minutes

Crusty bread, for the table

Remove tails from shrimp and discard.

Heat olive oil in deep skillet over medium heat. Add garlic and sauté 1 or 2 minutes, until garlic speaks by sizzling in oil.

Add wine and reduce by half. Add tomatoes and bring to a simmer. Add feta and stir constantly, until cheese melts into sauce. Add black pepper and oregano, stir to combine, and add raw shrimp. Cover and cook 5 minutes, stirring occasionally, until shrimp are pink and firm.

Add parsley and cooked, drained pasta to the shrimp and sauce. Serve immediately with warm, crusty bread.

Classic Garlic Shrimp

SERVES 4 TO 6

3 tablespoons extra-virgin olive oil (3 turns around the pan)

1 medium shallot, chopped fine

8 cloves garlic, minced

1/4 teaspoon (3 pinches) crushed red pepper flakes

1 bay leaf, fresh or dried

1 1/2 pounds jumbo shrimp, peeled and deveined

Coarse salt and black pepper, to taste

Juice of 1/2 lemon

2 tablespoons butter

1 cup dry white wine

4 sprigs fresh thyme, leaves stripped and chopped very fine

Grated zest of 1 lemon

A handful chopped fresh flat-leaf parsley

3 tablespoons butter, softened

1/4 cup grated Parmigiano or Romano cheese (2 handfuls)

6 crusty rolls, split

Heat a large skillet over medium to medium-high heat. Add oil and heat 1 minute. Add shallot. When shallot speaks by sizzling in oil, add garlic. When garlic speaks, add red pepper flakes and bay leaf and sauté, stirring constantly, for 1 minute more. Add shrimp and sprinkle with salt and pepper. Cook 3 minutes and transfer to platter. Remove bay leaf. Squeeze the juice of 1/2 lemon over shrimp.

Return pan to heat. Add butter. When butter melts, add wine and thyme. Bring wine to a boil and reduce liquid 1 minute. Pour sauce over shrimp and sprinkle with lemon zest and parsley.

Combine softened butter and grated cheese. Spread cheese butter on rolls and toast under hot broiler.

Serve shrimp with toasted bread for mopping up sauce and BLT Salad (recipe follows).

BLT Salad

SERVES 4 TO 6 AS A SIDE DISH OR APPETIZER, 2 AS AN ENTRÉE

6 slices center-cut bacon, or 1/2 pound sliced pancetta (Italian rolled, cured pork available at deli counter.)
2 small vine-ripe tomatoes
1 bunch arugula, stems removed, leaves washed and chopped (2 cups)
1 heart romaine lettuce, trimmed and coarsely chopped
Coarse salt and black pepper, to taste

DRESSING
1 small shallot, minced
1/3 cup extra-virgin olive oil (2 or 3 glugs)
2 to 3 tablespoons red wine vinegar (3 splashes)
1 teaspoon sugar (3 or 4 pinches)
Salt and black pepper, to taste

Chop bacon or pancetta into bite-size pieces and brown until crisp in a skillet over medium-high heat. Drain on paper towels and set aside.

Seed tomatoes and cut into bite-size wedges. Combine tomatoes with arugula and romaine in a large, shallow bowl. Sprinkle with bacon bits.

For dressing, place shallot in a small bowl and cover with oil. Heat in microwave on high for 1 minute or warm in a small pan on stove. Let stand 5 minutes to cool. Using a small whisk or a fork, combine oil and shallot with vinegar and sugar.

Season salad with salt and pepper and toss with dressing until evenly coated.

Shrimp Primavera with Bow Tie Pasta

SERVES 4 TO 6

This is the biggest palate-pleaser in the book.

2 tablespoons extra-virgin olive oil

2 tablespoons butter

1 carrot, peeled and cut into matchsticks

1/2 small red bell pepper, seeded and cut into matchsticks

1/2 small zucchini, cut into matchsticks

1/2 small yellow squash, cut into matchsticks

4 cloves garlic, chopped fine

1 pound large shrimp (26 to 30 per pound), peeled and deveined

1/2 cup clam juice

2 cups heavy (whipping) cream

3 pinches ground nutmeg (1/8 teaspoon)

2 pinches cayenne pepper

2 cups shredded basil leaves (60 leaves)

1 pound bow ties, cooked until al dente

Salt and black pepper, to taste

3 tablespoons pine nuts (pignoli), toasted

Put 1 tablespoon olive oil (1 turn of the pan) in a skillet set over medium heat. Add butter and melt into oil. Add vegetables and garlic. Cover pan and cook 5 minutes. Stir occasionally. Remove vegetables and return pan to heat, adding 1 tablespoon oil. Add shrimp and cook until pink and opaque. Remove shrimp and place pan back on heat. Add clam juice, cream, nutmeg, and cayenne to pan. Reduce until cream coats back of a spoon. Return vegetables and shrimp to pan and add basil.

Toss with pasta and season with salt and pepper to taste. Garnish with toasted pine nuts.

Quick Creole Shrimp

SERVES 4 GENEROUSLY

2 cups water

1 cup enriched white rice

2 tablespoons vegetable oil (twice around
the pan)

4 small stalks of celery with leaves from the
heart of stalk, chopped

1 medium onion, chopped

1 medium green bell pepper, seeded and
chopped

4 large cloves garlic, chopped

2 tablespoons flour (a palmful)

2 bay leaves, fresh or dried

2 sprigs fresh thyme, chopped, about
1 tablespoon, or 1 teaspoon dried thyme

1 can (28 ounces) diced tomatoes in their juice

3 to 4 dashes Worcestershire sauce (about 1
teaspoon)

6 to 8 dashes Tabasco or other cayenne pepper
sauce (about 2 teaspoons)

Coarse salt and black pepper, to taste

2 pounds large fresh shrimp, peeled and
deveined (see Note)

4 scallions, chopped, to garnish

Bring 2 cups water to a boil, add rice, and bring water back to a boil. Cover pot and reduce heat to low. Simmer 20 minutes, fluff rice with a fork, and remove from heat.

While rice cooks, place a deep skillet or heavy-bottomed pot on stovetop over medium to medium-high heat. Drizzle oil in a slow stream twice around the pan; heat oil and add celery, onion, green pepper, and garlic to pot. Cook veggies 5 minutes to soften and sweeten. Sprinkle pan with a palmful of flour, add bay and thyme leaves, and cook another 2 or 3 minutes. Stir in tomatoes, Worcestershire, Tabasco, and salt and pepper. Bring tomatoes to a bubble, then toss in shrimp. Partially cover pot by balancing pot cover on the rim so steam can escape. Allow shrimp to stew for 10 minutes in tomatoes, or until rice is done.

To serve, pour shrimp and sauce into shallow bowls. Using an ice cream scoop, scoop rice into balls and mound in the center of each bowlful of Creole shrimp. Sprinkle each bowl of shrimp and rice with a handful of chopped scallions. The rice is placed in the center of the bowl, rather then piling the Creole on top of a bed of rice. This prevents the rice from becoming bloated and mushy.

While I love this, my Nanny's Creole shrimp, you should know that there are as many ways to make this dish as there are Southern cooks—be creative; add chili powder, lemon juice, whatever floats your shrimp boat!

With a green salad and garlic toast, this is more than enough for 4 people.

Note: If you do not like to clean shrimp, peeled and deveined raw shrimp is available at many supermarkets; just ask your seafood manager for it. It's often not in the case, but they can get it for you.

Mystic-Style Portuguese Sea Scallops over Rice

SERVES 4

RICE

1 3/4 cups chicken broth
1 small white cooking onion, chopped fine
1 tablespoon butter
1 cup long-grain white rice

SCALLOPS

1 1/2 pounds large sea scallops
Coarse salt and black pepper, to taste
2 tablespoons extra-virgin olive oil
1/2 cup port or other sweet red wine
6 cloves garlic, minced
Juice of 1/2 lemon
A handful chopped fresh flat-leaf parsley

Bring chicken broth to a boil in a deep saucepan. Add onion, butter, and rice. Reduce heat to low and cover. Cook 20 minutes, stirring occasionally. Remove from heat and fluff with a fork when ready to serve.

Ten minutes before the rice is done, begin preparing scallops. Pat scallops dry and season lightly with a little salt and pepper. Heat oil in a heavy-bottomed skillet over high heat until very hot, until the oil begins to smoke. Add half the scallops to the pan and sear 2 minutes on each side till browned. Remove scallops to a warm oven (250 degrees) and repeat process with remaining scallops.

Return empty pan to medium heat and deglaze with port, scraping up all the good bits. Add garlic and sauté 30 seconds. Add scallops back to the pan and squeeze the juice of 1/2 lemon over them. Sprinkle scallops with parsley and serve over hot rice.

Bay Scallops with Rosemary

SERVES 4

1 1/2 pounds small bay scallops
Coarse salt and black pepper, to taste
2 tablespoons extra-virgin olive oil
2 sprigs fresh rosemary, leaves stripped
    from stem
2 bay leaves, fresh or dried

Get your scallops as dry as possible by draining in a colander, then placing on a paper towel-lined plate. Season scallops with salt and pepper.

Heat 1 tablespoon of olive oil in a heavy skillet over high heat until it is very hot. Add half the rosemary and 1 bay leaf. Heat oil and herbs 30 seconds. Add half the scallops to the pan and cook 2 minutes. Remove to warm platter and repeat process.

If the scallops still give off liquid, remove them after 3 minutes, reduce liquid till almost evaporated, then return scallops to pan for 1 minute more to coat in pan drippings.

You might want to serve this with a side dish of steamed new potatoes tossed with olive oil, salt, pepper, and parsley.

Angel-Hair Pasta with Scallops, Tomato, and Basil

SERVES 2 TO 3

1/4 cup extra-virgin olive oil (3 turns around
the pan)

5 cloves garlic, minced

1 pound bay scallops, drained very well

Salt and pepper, to taste

1 can (28 ounces) diced tomatoes, drained well

2 cups fresh basil leaves, cut into
thin strips

8 ounces angel-hair pasta, cooked until al dente

Place a large, heavy skillet over medium heat. Add oil and heat 1 minute. Add garlic and sauté 2 minutes, stirring constantly. Add scallops, season with salt and pepper, and cook 3 minutes, or till opaque. Add tomatoes and basil and heat through 1 minute. Remove from heat. Taste and adjust seasonings. Add pasta to pan and toss to combine well.

Linguini with Mussels

2 dozen mussels, scrubbed and beards
   pulled off
2 handfuls fresh flat-leaf parsley, large stems
   removed
1 medium onion, coarsely chopped
1/2 cup dry white wine

SAUCE

2 tablespoons extra-virgin olive oil (twice
   around the pan)
4 cloves garlic, minced
3 pinches crushed red pepper flakes
1 can (28 ounces) diced tomatoes, drained
A handful chopped fresh flat-leaf parsley
Coarse salt and black pepper, to taste
3/4 pound linguini, cooked until al dente

Place mussels, parsley, onion, and wine in a deep skillet and bring to a boil. Cover, reduce heat to medium, and steam 5 to 7 minutes, or until all mussels open. Discard any mussels that do not open. Drain mussels and reserve cooking liquid.

Return pan to medium heat. Add oil and heat. Add garlic and crushed pepper red flakes. When garlic speaks by sizzling in oil, add tomatoes and reserved liquid from mussels; cook 5 minutes. Add mussels and season with salt and pepper. Toss with hot pasta and top with parsley.

Linguini with Fresh Clam Sauce

SERVES 2 TO 3

36 littleneck clams, scrubbed well

2 cups dry white wine

1 medium onion, coarsely chopped

SAUCE

2 tablespoons extra-virgin olive oil (2 turns around the pan)

1 medium shallot, chopped fine

4 cloves garlic, minced

4 anchovy fillets, coarsely chopped

3 or 4 pinches crushed red pepper flakes

4 or 5 sprigs fresh thyme, leaves chopped (about 2 tablespoons)

4 ounces clam broth (half a bottle, can be found in canned fish aisle)

Coarse salt and black pepper, to taste

1/2 pound dried linguini, cooked until al dente

Zest of 1 lemon

A handful fresh flat-leaf parsley, chopped

Place clams, wine, and onion in a deep skillet and bring to a boil. Cover, reduce heat to medium, and steam until all of the clams open. Discard any clams that do not open. Drain clams and reserve the juice. Let clams cool. Using a seafood fork or small paring knife, remove 20 of the clams from their shells and chop coarsely.

Return skillet to medium heat. Add olive oil and heat. Add shallot, garlic, anchovies, and crushed red pepper flakes to hot oil. Cook until anchovies melt into oil. Add thyme leaves, reserved cooking liquid and clam juice. Season with a little salt and black pepper. Reduce liquids for 2 or 3 minutes. Add chopped clams, clams in shells, and drained, hot pasta. Remove pasta from heat and toss 1 or 2 minutes to allow pasta to absorb some of the juices.

Serve pasta in shallow bowls, arranging a few clams in their shells on top. Garnish bowls of pasta with lemon zest and parsley.

Steamed Clams or Mussels with Garlic Toast and Baby Greens Salad

SERVES 2 TO 3

1 tablespoon extra-virgin olive oil (1 turn around
the pan)
3 large shallots, chopped fine
4 cloves garlic, minced
3 pinches crushed red pepper flakes
4 sprigs fresh thyme (about 2 tablespoons),
chopped
1 1/2 cups dry white wine (4 glugs)
1/2 cup clam broth
2 dozen mussels, scrubbed and debearded, or
36 littleneck clams, scrubbed well
Salt and black pepper, to taste
A handful fresh flat-leaf parsley, chopped fine

Place a deep skillet over medium to medium-high heat. Add olive oil, shallots, garlic, crushed red pepper flakes, and thyme. Sauté 2 to 3 minutes, stirring constantly. Add wine and broth and bring to a boil. Add clams or mussels to pan, cover and steam until shells open. Discard any clams or mussels that do not open. Season with salt and pepper and sprinkle with parsley.

Garlic Toast (Bruschetta)

1 loaf chewy, crusty firm bread, sliced thin, on
an angle
4 cloves garlic, cracked from skin
Extra-virgin olive oil, for drizzling

Place bread slices on cookie sheet. Rub the slices on both sides with cracked garlic. Place the bread in a 450 degree F oven for 10 minutes, or until crisp and golden. Remove from oven and drizzle with extra-virgin olive oil.

Baby Greens Salad

3/4 pound mixed baby greens

4 ounces Asiago or Parmigiano cheese, shaved
    into thin slices

1 small shallot, minced

3 tablespoons extra-virgin olive oil

1 tablespoon white wine vinegar

2 pinches sugar

Salt and pepper, to taste

Toss greens and cheese shavings in a shallow bowl. Placed minced shallot in a small dish. Cover with olive oil and place in microwave. Heat oil on high for 45 seconds or warm in a small pan till shallot speaks or sizzles. Cool oil for 5 minutes, then combine with vinegar and sugar. Drizzle dressing over salad and season with salt and pepper to taste.

Spaghetti with Anchovies, Capers, and Bread Crumbs

SERVES 4 TO 6

1 pound dried spaghetti

6 tablespoons extra-virgin olive oil, total
1 large clove garlic, popped from skin with a
    whack against flat of knife
1 tin anchovies (8 to 10 fillets)
2 cups plain bread crumbs
Black pepper, to taste
4 cloves garlic, minced
3 ounces capers, drained, rinsed, and coarsely
    chopped
3 pinches crushed red pepper flakes
1/4 cup chopped fresh flat-leaf parsley
    (a couple of handfuls)
A couple pinches coarse salt

Bring a large pot of salted water to a boil. Add pasta and cook 6 to 8 minutes, until al dente—with a bite to it.

While pasta cooks, heat a large skillet over medium heat. Add 3 tablespoons oil (3 times around the pan) and the clove of cracked, whole garlic and sauté until garlic speaks in oil by sizzling. Add anchovies and cook until the fillets melt into oil. Add bread crumbs and toss with a wooden spoon until golden brown. Season with a few grinds of black pepper. Remove bread crumbs and set aside.

Return pan to heat and wipe clean with paper towel. Add remaining 3 tablespoons oil. Add chopped garlic, capers, and crushed red pepper flakes. Sauté 2 minutes. Add cooked, drained pasta to pan, add parsley, and toss with oil. Sprinkle half the crumbs over pasta in pan and toss. Season with a little coarse salt.

Transfer pasta to a serving platter and top with remaining crumbs. Serve with a tomato and onion salad and a good chianti.

Lobster and Linguini

SERVES 4

2 lobster tails (7 to 8 ounces each)

2 tablespoons butter

2 tablespoons extra-virgin olive oil (2 turns around the pan)

2 cloves garlic, crushed

3 pinches crushed red pepper flakes

1/2 cup dry white wine

1/2 cup heavy whipping cream

1 can (14 ounces) tomato sauce

Coarse salt and black pepper, to taste

1 pound egg or semolina fettuccini, cooked until al dente

A handful chopped fresh flat-leaf parsley

Starting at tail end of lobster, cut the underside of the tail lengthwise with scissors. Using a long, thin knife, scoop out meat. Dice lobster into bite-size pieces.

Heat a large skillet over medium heat. Add butter. When butter melts, add lobster and cook until red. Remove from pan. Return pan to heat and add oil, garlic, and crushed red pepper flakes. Cook garlic 2 minutes in oil, then remove. Add wine and reduce by half, 1 or 2 minutes. Add cream and lobster. Cook 5 minutes over reduced heat. Add tomato sauce and cook 5 minutes longer. Season with salt and pepper, to taste. Toss lobster and sauce with pasta and parsley and serve with a salad and bread.

Lobster and Angel-Hair Pasta
SERVES 2 TO 3

2 lobster tails (7 to 8 ounces each)
1/4 teaspoon saffron threads (2 or 3 pinches)
1/4 cup hot water
2 tablespoons butter
1 tablespoon extra-virgin olive oil (once around the pan)
1 medium shallot, chopped
1/2 cup dry sherry
1 cup heavy (whipping) cream
Zest of 1 lemon
Coarse salt and black pepper, to taste

1/2 pound angel-hair pasta, cooked until al dente

Cut lobster shell lengthwise on the underside using strong scissors and starting from tail end. Slide a long, thin knife between shell and meat and scoop out meat from shell. Cut lobster into bite-size pieces.

Soak saffron threads in hot water.

Heat a large skillet over medium heat and add butter. When butter melts, add lobster and cook until meat turns red. Remove from pan and set aside. Return pan to heat. Add oil and shallot. Cook 2 minutes. Add sherry to pan and reduce for 1 or 2 minutes. Add cream, lemon zest, and saffron, discarding soaking water. Reduce heat and simmer 5 minutes, or until sauce coats back of spoon. Season lightly with salt and pepper. Add lobster and heat a minute longer. Toss pasta with a little sauce and place on platter or dinner plates. Spoon remaining sauce and lobster over pasta and serve.

Seafood Newburg
SERVES 4

2 lobster tails (7 to 8 ounces each)

3 tablespoons butter, total

1/2 pound lump crabmeat (ask at seafood counter of market)

2 tablespoons all-purpose flour (a handful)

1/2 teaspoon paprika (3 or 4 pinches)

1/8 teaspoon cayenne pepper (a couple of pinches)

A few pinches coarse salt

1 pint (2 cups) half-and-half

2 large egg yolks, beaten

2 tablespoons dry sherry (a splash)

6 slices white bread, toasted and lightly buttered

Cut shells of lobster tails on the underside with strong scissors, starting at narrow end of tail. Loosen and remove meat using a long, thin knife. Cut lobster into bite-size pieces.

Heat a large skillet over medium heat. Melt 2 tablespoons butter in pan and add lobster meat and crab. Cook until lobster turns red. Remove seafood from pan and return pan to heat. Add remaining 1 tablespoon butter. When butter melts, add flour and season with paprika, cayenne, and a couple pinches salt. Whisk in flour until a smooth paste forms. Continue whisking while adding half-and-half to pan. Cook, stirring constantly, until sauce thickens.

Stir a few spoonfuls of the hot cream sauce into the beaten egg yolks. Add egg yolks to sauce, stirring constantly. Add seafood back to pan and coat evenly with sauce. Remove from heat and stir in a splash of sherry.

To serve, cut toast corner to corner in points. Arrange points on platter or dinner plates and spoon seafood over the toast points.

Index